T0258789

Leading High-Reliability Organizations in Healthcare

Leading High-Reliability Organizations in Healthcare

Richard Morrow

CRC Press
Taylor & Francis Group
Boca Raton London New York

CRC Press is an imprint of the
Taylor & Francis Group, an **informa** business
A PRODUCTIVITY PRESS BOOK

CRC Press
Taylor & Francis Group
6000 Broken Sound Parkway NW, Suite 300
Boca Raton, FL 33487-2742

© 2016 by Taylor & Francis Group, LLC
CRC Press is an imprint of Taylor & Francis Group, an Informa business

No claim to original U.S. Government works

Printed on acid-free paper
Version Date: 20160113

International Standard Book Number-13: 978-1-4665-9488-3 (Hardback)

Visit the Taylor & Francis Web site at
http://www.taylorandfrancis.com

and the CRC Press Web site at
http://www.crcpress.com

Contents

Note from the Author

High reliability is achieved when the top leadership supports the entire organization in achieving and sustaining reliability. The leaders can do this by setting the vision, creating the culture, and supporting the infrastructure, especially in sponsoring facilitators who are skilled in reliability and will translate high reliability for everyone inside and outside the organization. High reliability must transcend the organization into its suppliers and into the postdischarge care organizations such as skilled nursing facilities, rehabilitation sites, and homes that support the patient and family. For some organizations, such as ambulatory surgical centers, the time spent within the surgical center may be less than the time spent preparing for the surgery and after the surgery.

The Institute of Medicine, the Centers for Medicare & Medicaid Services (CMS), The Joint Commission (TJC), and other regulatory or accrediting bodies have stressed the urgency of transforming hospitals into places where each patient receives the best-quality care every single time. Hospital leaders agree that they need to change their leadership focus, resources, and systems and processes in order to achieve substantial increases in reliability. Leadership is the most important variable because high-reliability methods, cultures, and concepts have been in place for years that are now proven to work in healthcare.

This book builds on my first books, *Utilizing the 3Ms of Process Improvement in Healthcare* (2012)[1] and *Utilizing the 3Ms of Process Improvement* (2012).[2] These books provide more depth and skill for suppliers and those in healthcare who need to understand and gain capability, stability, and performance in their measurement systems and healthcare products. These skills are critical because healthcare will never achieve its potential reliability without high reliability in its suppliers (supplies including implants such as orthopedic implants), and all upstream and downstream stakeholders.

I have enjoyed being able to help hundreds of organizations, yet we still have touched only the surface of healthcare. This is why I wrote my first two books, and now this is the next step in achieving high reliability.

This book presents concepts and tools that a growing number of hospitals are using to help achieve their safety, quality, and efficiency goals. Most importantly, I share in detail the concepts and tools that the vast majority of healthcare providers, including their suppliers, are still not using.

If you think that this book is just about reliability of safety in healthcare, you are in for a bonus. Reliability, from a customer's or patient's perspective, is usually about performance and specifically clinical outcomes. Clinical outcomes are achievements, such as the time that it takes to return to a function that is measured; for instance, how well a total knee replacement reduces pain and improves mobility or an open-heart surgical patient's present ability to live a robust life again with energy and without pain. Fortunately, more and more agencies, including CMS, Blue Cross Blue Shield, and TJC, and the public are promoting healthcare to becoming a high-reliability organization for years. Unfortunately, some have interpreted high reliability myopically as an organization that does not harm its customers. Reliability in healthcare should be much more than not hurting our patients and staff.

> Reliability is achieving favorable outcomes safely
> through the life cycle.
>
> **Rick Morrow**

We choose goods and services that we believe will achieve the intended outcomes. I purchase automobiles primarily based on getting my family and me to where we need to go without failure for years to come. We can see the statistics on which cars have the best reliability. Car companies compete on the basis of reliability.

My purpose in writing this book is to accelerate healthcare and achieve higher reliability. To accomplish this mission, I share roles, responsibilities, skills, and tools for leaders, providers, staff, and suppliers. I purposely do not mention a responsibility of patients in preventing mistakes and advocates to be very clear that high-reliability organizations take prime responsibility for delivering services reliably and safely. I believe it is wrong to deflect responsibility onto the patient—for instance, when healthcare devotes more energy and resources to telling patients to speak up if care-givers do not wash their hands than it does to ensuring the creation of an environment in which everyone washes their hands. True, patients can contribute to injury while under our roofs and might not take their medicines post discharge, contributing to their readmission, but the companies I have worked for, such as in electrical safety products, believed that our role should be to deliver value and protect the customers who use our product. We used techniques that I share in this book building on techniques that I first defined in my previous books. Yet this book alone should result in significantly better clinical outcomes and safer care. The key is to predict outcomes, continuously improve them, and control processes including human interactions to sustain.

Successes in healthcare reliability are shared similar to the development and manufacture of today's ground fault circuit protector device at Eaton Electrical, which provides uninterrupted power in the home until the homeowner mistakenly drops a hair dryer into the sink. To blame the customers for a risky act and claim no responsibility for electrocution is not what high-reliability organizations practice.

I hope that every leader in healthcare learns the techniques in this book and continues learning high-reliability practices. If leadership does not value learning about high reliability, we have little hope in achieving it. Therefore, I've included the business case for higher reliability in later chapters. In addition to the idea that better clinical outcomes and preventing harm are the right things to do, high-reliability organizations may find higher profits and margins because of the loyalty that is built from reliable and safe outcomes. I specifically cover how to achieve higher patient experience scores and margins because healthcare is just now beginning to have to compete for quality and safety as many other industries have had to do for centuries.

The good news is that achieving higher reliability is not a secret. This book is among many that are dedicated to improving reliability. Yet, I have very short conversations, if any, among many healthcare leaders, providers, staff, and suppliers around reliability. The term high-reliability organizations is getting more and more airplay. This is a start to promoting what is needed in healthcare. How to achieve higher reliability is what this book and my prior two books address. We know that high reliability can be achieved. We know that it takes years, and we know that we want it in healthcare.

Let us start utilizing the 3Ms by measuring reliability, managing to the measure every day, and making it easier for leaders, providers, staff, and suppliers to achieve it.

References

1. Morrow, R. *Utilizing the 3Ms of Process Improvement in Healthcare*, Boca Raton, FL: CRC Press/Taylor & Francis Group, 2012.
2. Morrow, R. *Utilizing the 3Ms of Process Improvement*, Boca Raton, FL: CRC Press/Taylor & Francis Group, 2012.

Features

- We include the roles and responsibilities of the two organizational components in achieving high reliability: (1) leadership and (2) the reliability engineers who apply reliability methods both technically and socially throughout the value stream of healthcare. Please allow me to use the term *engineer* for those who learn and apply the science of reliability even though they may not be schooled in reliability nor an engineer. What is key is the passion to learn and to apply.
- Leading without engineering and engineering without leading eliminate any chance of achieving the high reliability that healthcare can achieve.

The space shuttle *Challenger* catastrophe could have been prevented if leadership had listened to Morton Thiokol engineers. NASA leadership was responsible because it held the decision-making authority. Retired engineer, Bob Ebeling recalls, "Had they listened to me and wait(ed) for a weather change, it might have been a completely different outcome." "30 Years After Explosion, Challenger Engineer Still Blames Himself," National Public Radio interview aired 1/28/2016.

■ My request is for both leaders and reliability engineers to read this book from cover to cover for a shared understanding of what each role must accomplish and why. A common understanding leads to a shared appreciation of each other's recommendations and thus more likely better decisions and behaviors for higher reliability. Knowing that each other's interests vary in terms of detail within each role, we highlight the areas of detail for each role so that the reader of interest may more quickly refer back when leading or designing reliability improvement.

■ Case studies of both high reliability and failures permeate this book because we believe that history does repeat itself. The leaders in reliability are students of history and believe that learning the mistakes of the past and mindfulness in the present and future are a first step toward higher reliability.

■ Reliability is defined in Chapter 1 with the culture of high-reliability organizations discussed in Chapter 4. Shared throughout the book are the necessary infrastructure, methods, and analytics to achieve higher reliability and to sustain it, for without sustaining reliability, there is no reliability.

■ Leadership principles are critical in becoming, sustaining, and improving high-reliability organizations, for it is the leadership in healthcare that must now focus on reliability, resource it, and reinforce it as healthcare begins to compete on quality.

■ Reliability engineers will learn the methods and analytics and how to communicate with leaders in achieving higher reliability.

■ Included in this book are case studies of achieving higher reliability within healthcare, some achieving zero defects for years. Because many key elements of a high-reliability organization are missing or still void in healthcare, I added case studies that are relevant to healthcare and that give insight to our healthcare sites of the future. Graphics and illustrations share visually the look of a high-reliability healthcare organization.

One will be able to sense a high-reliability organization by walking and interacting in its processes.

Author

Rick Morrow, MBA, MBB, is an author and executive with 30 years of experience in high-reliability organizations and healthcare. His personal mission is to help healthcare achieve high reliability in clinical outcomes and safety. Morrow's work includes writing a series of books, utilizing the 3Ms of process improvement, which includes *Utilizing the 3Ms of Process Improvement in Healthcare: A Roadmap to High Reliability Using Lean, Six Sigma, and Change Leadership.* He is a contributing editor to healthcare quality and safety manuals, including the *Safe Surgery Guide*, Joint Commission Resources; *Hand-Off Communications*, Joint Commission Resources; and *Patient Flow*, Joint Commission Resources.

Morrow recently joined CHRISTUS Health to continue his mission in helping healthcare achieve higher reliability. When he first worked with CHRISTUS, one of the top 10 largest nonprofit healthcare systems in the United States, he led the pay-for-performance work during the clinical integration with MedAssets and was the VP of Quality, Safety, Reliability, and Patient Experience. Morrow developed the Six Sigma and High Reliability training system deployed in healthcare organizations across the United States and United Kingdom. CHRISTUS has proven that zero harm, better patient experiences, and improved financial margins are possible. Morrow developed the performance improvement targeting system used by CHRISTUS and with clients to maximize quality, safety, patient experience, and financial gains in pay-for-value programs, including Centers for Medicare & Medicaid Services' (CMS) value-based purchasing, excess readmissions, and healthcare.

Morrow's experience includes leading quality and reliability as an executive in healthcare, electrical safety, first responder communication products, aerospace, and aviation. His global experience has included Eaton Corporation; SKF, a world leader in reliability; Motorola, where he wrote much of the Toyota Production System into Motorola's Six Sigma program; and United Airlines.

Dr. Mark Chassin, president of The Joint Commission (TJC), recruited Morrow to lead the launch of performance improvement at TJC. Morrow simultaneously led the startup and first successes in TJC's Center for Transforming Healthcare. He wrote and developed TJC's Robust Process Improvement (RPI), a blend of Lean, Six Sigma, and Change Leadership. RPI is credited with being the methodology of choice by the Center for Transforming Healthcare in its quality improvements with Johns Hopkins, Memorial Hermann, Cedars-Sinai, and other leading institutions. RPI was the methodology used in eliminating wrong-site surgery, infections, and improving hand-off communications. Morrow's team developed TJC's Targeted Solutions Tool, a web-based performance improvement system used by many TJC-accredited organizations to make performance improvement a step-by-step improvement methodology.

Morrow developed and launched Penn Medicine's Performance Improvement in Action with Kristi Pintar, director at Penn Medicine; HCA International's Leadership and Lean Six Sigma Program; and High Reliability courses used across the United States and United Kingdom to reduce readmissions and eliminate surgical site infections and healthcare-acquired conditions of harm.

He earned a Motorola Certified Master Black Belt certification with certifications in Lean, Six Sigma, Change Leadership, and Supply Chain. He earned his MBA at the University of Illinois Executive Program.

Chapter 1

Reliability— Ability to Rely

Leadership and Engineering Reliability

Healthcare needs to become more reliable and will be when the concepts in this book are in place, as they are in organizations that have achieved reliable outcomes. But, what is this term High Reliability healthcare is using and what does it mean to become a High Reliability Organization? When I first joined healthcare, I was surprised to hear the term *high reliability*. Adding the adjective high to describe reliability is redundant. Either we have reliability or we do not. Granted, one system could be more reliable than another, but who is to say what is "high"? Is the reliability in aviation higher than the reliability in aerospace? That is like asking if the food in California is fresher than the food in Florida. The question cannot be answered, and thus it does not make any sense to even ask it. Adding high in front of reliability is popular, especially in healthcare. Used in our flexible definition, the adjective high might be used as a modifier of expected, for example, better performance to expectations. Better compared to what, though? Is high really needed to describe organizations that achieve reliability or a longer duration of the expected outcome? Maybe longer is not better.

Alas, the term high reliability is too profusely used now in healthcare to rein it in. I guess that we should be thankful that healthcare is speaking reliability now more than ever because the popularity is having the desired effect, as evidenced by the number of presentations referencing high reliability at healthcare conferences.*

I realized also that high reliability was used to describe how safe healthcare is. No one used the term high reliability in regard to how well treatments and surgical procedures improved patient function that is sustained over time. It seemed that those leaders preaching high reliability in healthcare were concerned mostly with safety—in other words, not hurting people. Clinical outcomes were not included in the conversation.

Achieving reliability in healthcare must start with understanding what reliability is, how to measure it, and then how to improve it in an organization. Achieving reliability takes an organization, not just a leader or a frontline staff member. That brings us to the often-heard statement that healthcare needs to become a high-reliability organization (HRO). I will cover HROs in a later chapter.

Reliability in outcomes and safety are absolutely necessary in healthcare due to the many risks that are associated with caring for health. Risks arise. Thus, I created the framework to understand reliability in outcomes and safety shown in Figure 1.1. I will share how the reliability of outcomes is related to the reliability of safety. Reliability is only achieved when one understands that any one process is only a portion of a system. To achieve high reliability, we need to take a systems approach. Reliability is not achieved by improving one process alone when healthcare's complexity can be defined by the many processes that are involved in patient care.

---

* Institute for Healthcare Improvement Conference held in 2014 in Orlando, Florida.

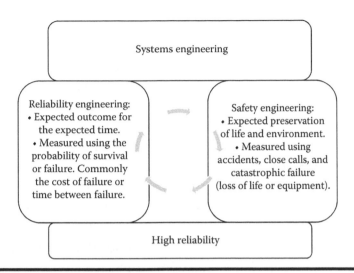

Figure 1.1   Framework of high reliability.

We engineer reliability in both the operation of the process and in the system's safety. Safety is necessary for both life and environment. In other words, high reliability requires reliability engineering and safety engineering. I hope that this framework helps in understanding that reliability comes from a systems approach, and high reliability is an outcome of sufficient reliability and safety engineering.

Higher reliability is needed in clinical outcomes. The U.S. Department of Health and Human Services reported that a preliminary cumulative total of 1.3 million fewer healthcare-acquired conditions (HACs), otherwise known as harm to the patients, were experienced over the years 2011, 2012, and 2013.[1] "I prefer the term hospital-aquired conditions" over the more narrow term hospital-acquired conditions because of the need to look at healthcare as a system—not just a hospital. I often find a hospital-acquired condition is a result of variables before and after admission to a hospital. This equates to 121 HACs per 1000 discharges. Many of us have examples of a lack of reliability in healthcare. The most unfortunate are those who have lost their lives in our healthcare processes unnecessarily. Preventable mortality is perhaps one of the gravest reliability measures.

Peter Pronovost wrote in 2010 that, although only 1 in 20 inpatient deaths are really preventable despite the statistics that are used, 31,000 patients died unnecessarily in intensive care units due to bloodstream infections, which are entirely preventable.[2]

A member of my family underwent an elective cardiology procedure to cure a cardiac arrhythmia. After much preparation, including wearing a heart monitor, numerous images taken, surgery, and much pain, there was no improvement in the arrhythmia. Fortunately, the condition of our loved one was not worse at discharge unlike what happens to many other patients considering the potential of a HAC.

Another key measure of reliability, other than preventable mortality, is preventable readmission—a readmission that is much broader in definition than readmission to an acute care hospital. A readmission could be considered any additional action that is needed due to a failure in the original procedure. This can be a return to the emergency room (ER) after discharge from the ER due to excessive bleeding that is caused by a poor wound closure or a return trip to the pharmacy for a different drug because the first-prescribed drug did not have the intended effect. Our mission is to apply reliability methods to improve the reliability of clinical processes. Until we achieve higher levels of process reliability, we will forever need to focus on the reliability of safety.

One of the most reliable products is in every home, office, factory, airplane, and most new cars. This product has become so reliable that we only *bother with it* after it has saved our building or us from harm. It is called an electrical circuit breaker. We expect the circuit breakers in our house to *trip* if an electrical hazard occurs. When, if ever, have you experienced a circuit breaker itself to not reliably function? These devices are amazing in the energy and heat that occur during an electrical fault and yet can be reset again and again. The companies that produce circuit breakers compete on reliability. Those that have failed in reliability do not exist. In addition to the competition that forces these firms out of the industry, there are independent testing organizations such as

Underwriters Laboratories that have validated the reliability of circuit breakers for all manufacturers using outcome measures that are important to us, the users. Outcomes measures, such as the time it takes the breaker to open the circuit, are critical in protecting the wiring to avoid fires and preventing electrical shock. This is a time-based measure. Another measure is how many years the circuit breaker will function before it fails.

I imagine that this next outcome measure is easy for you to relate to healthcare, if you have not already associated the tripping outcome to a trauma patient getting treatment such as vitamin K injections to stop the bleeding. Circuit breaker manufacturers design a breaker to trip, and then to be reset to close the circuit, allowing electricity to flow after a risk has been eliminated. The benefit to homeowners is simply switching the breaker back on versus having to replace a fuse that is destroyed after performing the task of opening the circuit. Thus, a required outcome measure is how many times a breaker can turn on and off before wearing out and failing to open or close the circuit. This is an example of a quality-based metric versus time-based.

Clinical Outcomes—Return to Function

Clinical outcomes should be patient centric. One measure gaining in popularity is measuring the time to return to function. I think about how long our blood vessels stay open after a cardiac procedure opens the vessel or how long a knee replacement lasts.

In healthcare, we do not see measures of clinical outcomes nearly as much as we see measures of how much or little harm patients experience.

Where are the measures as to which surgeons, implants, and healthcare organizations provide the most reliable clinical outcomes? The Centers for Medicare & Medicaid Services (CMS) has started to measure and financially reward healthcare organizations that are above the national median in processes of care, mortality, safety, efficiency, and patient experience. Yet, all of these measures, except patient experience measures, are about not hurting the customers—not about how reliable our clinical outcome was. Safety is a given in the eyes of patients, yet, unfortunately, healthcare does need to focus intently on safety as well as reliable clinical outcomes. Thus, we will cover in detail how to achieve safe *and* reliable processes resulting in improved clinical outcomes.

Until we get clinical care right the first time, we increase the probability of harm and thus perpetuate the need to focus on safety. High reliability as a term in healthcare has been hijacked to focus only on safety. There are entire firms that are dedicated to higher reliability in safety for patients and staff. These firms typically promote the increase in reportable events very early on. This is valid, and I suggest that reporting events should be mandatory. The underreporting of safety concerns is widespread and a known issue in healthcare, and we know that staff do not report all of the safety issues and thus miss opportunities to improve safety. The reason for this underreporting is often due to a lack of a just culture which leads to a lack in reporting. Starting an effort to improve safety often results in more events being recorded as the culture shifts to one of a just culture[3] and leadership promotes openness and sharing.

High reliability in safety is not what our customers are most interested in, however. It is not why I go to healthcare.

> Patient: I come to healthcare for wellness. I expect that no one will hurt me.

We will never break out of this cycle of predominantly focusing on safety until we achieve high reliability in clinical care. Using the measure of reported events makes this clearer. In the following chart, I share the actual data on the frequency of reported events in the perioperative processes including events occurring during the surgery at a very high volume healthcare organization. See Figure 1.2.

In Figure 1.2, we see how the actual number of safety concerns increased at the start of the project, and then diminished to an actual very low number of events occurring, and thus there is no need to report. This chart counts the actual events, not just what was reported. High reliability demands leadership. The chief executive officer and the chair of surgery both led the effort. They made it clear that the organization needed to focus on the reliability of the surgical processes to achieve reliably safe surgeries. Making the process more reliable, that is, reducing the risks and defects all along the process, is the best way to increase the reliability of a safe surgery.

The issue is that the healthcare organizations are left short of help if they do not learn the reliability concepts in this book that reduce the events.

Improving the reliability of clinical care and outcomes is the way to lead organizations to high reliability.

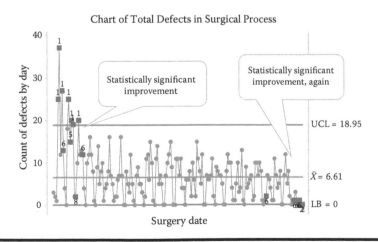

Figure 1.2   Reported events in eliminating wrong patient, site, or side surgeries.

Reliability Defined

There are many definitions of reliability. Some seem useful, some are incorrect confusing reliability with having standard work, and too many definitions are too limiting to support achieving high reliability. Before I share my definition of reliability, what is yours? Take a minute and write it. Consider sharing your initial definition on my website http://www.rpmexec.com/reliability/initialdefinitions.

Did you include a synonym of reliability, such as dependable or good? Or, maybe you defined reliability by using an antonym, such as dodginess, questionable, or uncertainness?

In healthcare, many consider reliability to mean safe. Reliability is much more than a term for safety, as is too often considered in healthcare. A patient should expect not to be harmed, but reliability in healthcare must be much more than a safe place.

I see businesses that state that their number-one goal is to have a safe workplace. Throughout this book, I want us to keep focused on the customers when we discuss reliability. I have never met a customer who buys a service or product from me because I lead a safe place to work. They might have been buying products that keep them safe, such as at Eaton Cutler-Hammer, where we build circuit breakers with a primary function to protect the wiring in your home knowing that fire from overheated wires is dangerous to property and lives. Thus, you want reliability in the circuit breakers. To be clear, the customers are not paying me to have a safe workplace for the associates who build the breakers; they are purchasing a product to provide safety. True, some may not buy my products if they believe that I do not provide a safe workplace, as consumers have protested against companies in third-world countries.

Reliability is not just capability. We will discuss capability first because understanding what capability is adds to our understanding of the two elements in the definition of reliability.

Capability, according to the *Merriam-Webster Dictionary*, is defined as "the facility or potential for an indicated use or deployment."[4] The word *potential* seems problematic in a definition of reliability. What if we said to a patient that our potential to not harm you is 80%? Thus, capability is not exactly what we are looking for when we consider reliable healthcare.

The Automotive Industry Action Group is one of the best and most widely used sources of quality and reliability concepts. In the *Statistical Process Control Reference Manual*,[2] the authors defined process capability and process performance. They state that "Process capability is determined by the variation that comes from common causes" (p. 19). Thus, reliability is much more than capability. Capability can be achieved in any process that has low variation. A surgical procedure that always results in profuse bleeding has low variation in terms of excessive bleeding. Capability is not enough.

Process performance is closer to what customers want. It is the overall output of the process and how it relates to their requirements (defined by specifications), irrespective of the process variation.

So far, we know that reliability needs to be something more than standard work. Achieving process capability's understanding and achieving low variation are not enough. Process performance adds the requirements of the customers or specification, so we are getting closer to what reliability is.

When we add a time dimension to process performance, it leads us to defining reliability, a universal definition regardless of industry. It is also a definition that fits an organization, which is to become a high-reliability organization in healthcare—a truly highly reliable provider of care.

Reliability: Getting the Expected Outcome throughout the Expected Time

One sees this definition fitting any endeavor. We may substitute other words for *expected* making this definition fit both initial designs and ongoing products and services. In designing a system, service, or product, we could exchange expected with *designed* or *intended*. What we must always do is to include both elements of reliability: outcome and time.

Reliability, we must understand, should not be claimed without understanding the process capability. Process capability is understanding the process performance, including its variation in achieving the requirements for some amount of time. And, until the process is stable, any claim to capability is false. We will understand better about stability and control in other chapters. For now, please understand that reliability requires stability.

Another dimension in defining reliability is the error potential in our calculation of reliability. Measuring reliability should be conservative in that we acknowledge our imperfect knowledge of the future. The reliability of a service or product yet to fail is a prediction. Thus, we put parameters around the expectations by adding the *probability* of survival or failure at a given time. For example, we expect 89% of the implants to continue functioning throughout the first 15 years. We could add a confidence level, such as 95%, as well. The reliability statement would read, "We have a 95% confidence level that 89% of the implants will function to specification throughout the first 15 years post operative."

The Commonwealth Fund report, *Mirror, Mirror on the Wall, 2014 Update: How the U.S. Health Care System Compares Internationally*, shares, "The United States health care system is the most expensive in the world, ... the U.S. underperforms relative to other countries on most dimensions of performance" (p. 1).[5] See Figure 1.3. "Among the 11 nations studied in this report—Australia, Canada, France, Germany, the Netherlands, New Zealand, Norway, Sweden, Switzerland, the United Kingdom, and the United States—the U.S. ranks last, as it did in the 2010, 2007, 2006, and 2004 editions of *Mirror, Mirror*. Most troubling, the U.S. fails to achieve better health outcomes than the other countries" (p. 1).[5]

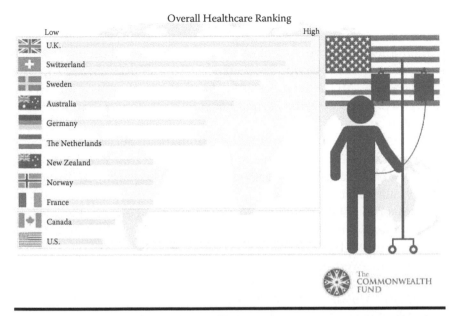

Figure 1.3   Commonwealth Fund report across nations. (From Davis, K. et al., *Mirror, Mirror on the Wall: How the Performance of the U.S. Health Care System Compares Internationally, 2014 Update.* **The Commonwealth Fund, June 2014. Available at http://www.common wealthfund.org/publications/fund-reports/2014/jun/mirror-mirror.)**

And, for those who think that there is a firewall protecting U.S. healthcare organizations from offshore competition with the argument that one cannot outsource emergency care, look no further than the number of surgical procedures that are performed outside of the country where the patient resides. A *New England Journal of Medicine* article, "Will the surgical world become flat?" by Arnold Milstein and Mark Smith, relates the U.S. car market in the 1960s to healthcare today. "But how many observers in the 1960s thought that Japan would come to dominate the U.S. car market or China U.S. textiles? Even if the offshore surgical market appears limited, it might become important in communities with more low-income recent immigrants. It also might influence national efforts to understand why care in the United States costs and grows so much. Finally, as telemedicine progresses, the adage that 'all health care is local' will recede" (p. 4).[6]

References

1. Efforts to improve patient safety result in 1.3 million fewer patient harms. *Agency for Healthcare Research and Quality*, Rockville, MD, November 2015. Available at http://www.ahrq .gov/professionals/quality-patient-safety/pfp/interimhacrate2013 .html
2. Statistical Process Control Reference Manual, Second Edition. Issued July 2005. Available at http://www.hopkinsmedicine.org /news/media/releases/death_rates_not_best_judge_of_hospital _quality_researchers_say.
3. Reason, J. 1997. *Managing the Risks of Organizational Accidents.* Surrey, UK: Ashgate.
4. Merriam-Webster Online Dictionary, Copyright 2015 by Merriam-Webster, Incorporated.
5. Davis, K., Stremikis, K., Schoen, C., and Squires, D. 2014. *Mirror, Mirror on the Wall, 2014 Update: How the U.S. Health Care System Compares Internationally.* The Commonwealth Fund, June. Available at http://www.commonwealthfund.org /publications/fund-reports/2014/jun/mirror-mirror.
6. Milstein, A. and Smith, M. 2007. Will the surgical world become flat? *Health Affairs*, 26, no. 1, 137–141.

Chapter 2

Measuring Reliability

461 days since our last central line–associated bloodstream infection!
  A beautifully simple measure of reliability.

Introduction

My purpose in this chapter is to build an appreciation of the science of reliability. It is not my intention to cover all of the concepts that are used in organizations that have been used in achieving high reliability. I have used these concepts in achieving zero defects for years in a variety of industries and now in healthcare where they are just as necessary. I ask you to at least browse the math and read the entire text because I will cover what differentiates highly reliable organizations from many in healthcare. In fact, there are some concepts in this chapter that are universally applied outside of healthcare, and not once have I met a person applying them in healthcare—yet.

Consider this chapter a sample of reliability measurement, not an all-inclusive source of mathematical formulae. At the end of this chapter I will share a reference of a textbook on reliability that covers most, if not all, of healthcare's needs.[1]

Measuring reliability, however, does not need to be complex for some situations. Counting the days since the last failure is a very effective measure of reliability. We will start using *days since last infection* after we have improved healthcare processes to having infrequent failures. We may have applied some of the more advanced reliability measures in the processes to achieve relatively infrequent infections. And, we would have placed controls preventing failure before we recommend using this simple measure.

Common Measures of Reliability

Clinical Outcome Measures Important to the Patient

Imagine walking into an airplane and on the cabin door seeing an outcome metric like we have in healthcare: "12 days since the last aborted landing." "200 days since the last food poisoning." We would never even think of seeing a chart like this. But, here is what one can see in most hospitals: "432 days since the last catheter-associated urinary tract infection."

Here is what I would post if I really wanted to compete:

"Our elective total knee patients are able to walk unassisted in one day—two times faster than our competition." "Our patients go home 20% faster after heart surgery with 30% higher thoracic capacity."

Just looking at what high-reliability organizations (HROs) measure and what most healthcare organizations measure gives a hint of how much farther we have to go in healthcare in becoming an HRO. Let us learn the most common measures that are used in reliability to appreciate what leaders and staff in HROs measure.

Days since Last Failure

This simple measure of reliability is used in healthcare to share how many days it has been since the last unfavorable episode of whatever is being measured. I suggest this measure often such as when we are reducing infections and other healthcare-acquired conditions. At CHRISTUS[2] Santa Rosa Medical Center, the team achieved more than 400 days of perfect compliance in managing urinary catheters. There is evidence that the risk of infection increases significantly after two days of catheter usage. Compliance to the measure is to remove and document the removal of the urinary catheter within two days of surgery or document a reason not to remove. The Centers for Medicare & Medicaid Services (CMS) refers to this measure as SCIP-9. SCIP is an acronym for surgical care improvement project. The SCIP measures were formed to improve the reliability and safety of surgical patients.

Rate of Failure

The count of failures divided by a count of events often is enough to incite action. An example is in the laboratory process. Let us say that out of 100 blood sample vials, we find 2 on average to be defective. The rate of failure is 2%. In other words, blood sample vials fail on average at the rate of 2 in every 100 vials.

$$\frac{2 \text{ failures}}{100 \text{ vials}} = 0.02 = 2\%$$

The vacuum loss in blood sample tubes occurs too often. In an annual physical exam I had a few years ago, the phlebotomist had a difficult time drawing blood because the first sample vial would not fill with my blood. He explained that this is a frequent occurrence and was caused by the tube losing its vacuum. I asked him if he was working on the issue, and he replied "no" without hesitation. I asked further questions, hoping that someone was working on the reliability of the tubes, and no action seemed to be occurring, nor even a desire.

Notice that the example above does not have a critical element in the definition of reliability: time. This is okay if the purpose is to understand the probability of getting a defective vial. Let us add to the example the element of time, which brings us to a reliability measure.

Mean Time to Failure and Mean Time between Failures

High-reliability organizations are highly reliable because they have found ways to improve the capability of their services and to extend the time between failures. In automotive, we were having early failures of components. Some failures occurred before the vehicle left the assembly plant where our components were installed. These modes of failure are called *zero-kilometer* failures because the vehicle had essentially no mileage on it before the failure occurred. The reliability of these components is considered very poor because of the short time between failures. The components worked at our plant but failed soon after. Our definition of time at the component supplier was the time from production or shipment until the component failed. The voice of our customers could include a less granular measure of reliability, and that is the number of days between failures. In other words, they might want us to show the days between failures, and the goal would be to achieve zero failures eventually and interim goals of extending the days between failures.

Let us look at reliability from the component manufacturer's perspective and measurement system first and then how the automotive assembly plant customers might perceive and measure it.

At Motorola, I volunteered to help the team improve the reliability of OnStar. OnStar is an amazing device that does many things for the driver and passengers, including an option to automatically call for help if the vehicle air bag deploys. It is a cell phone, sensor system, alerting system, and more. OnStar and similar technologies, including BMW's Assist, are called telematics units—an appropriate name because of the telecommunications and automatic functions that occur through the device. If the air bag deploys, we assume that the vehicle has been in an accident, and help may be needed. Time can be of the essence in saving the lives of the passengers and the driver, and OnStar is a telecommunications device that includes cellular communication. In an accident severe enough for the air bag to deploy, the driver and the passengers may be incapacitated to request for help. If the air bag deploys, OnStar wakes up from a power-saving state, calls 911, and prepares to transmit Global Positioning System coordinates for the first responders. This waking-up mode is common in most, if not all, cellular devices, and is useful to preserve battery life while the device is not needed.

The issue with OnStar years ago was that it may *not* wake up. Even though the OnStar system passed tests at the manufacturing site, it may not wake up in tests at the vehicle assembly plant, and this failure mode causes a zero-kilometer failure. To think that the device failed so early in its life is unnerving because the actual environment of use for the car or truck will be often much more stressful such as vibration on rough roads, extreme temperatures, and the longer life cycles of automobiles today; thanks to the longer life cycles of their components. Zero-kilometer failures are thus very concerning.

The good news is that zero-kilometer failures make it easier to find the root causes and solve the issue. The reason is that these failures happen so soon after we make the device while the *trail is still warm*. Key is to also utilize the 3Ms (measure, manage to the measure, and make it easier to do the right thing) in a timely manner. HROs have leaders who value timely data. What we found at the manufacturing site was a lack of real-time test data between the end of the manufacturing process where the *wake up* feature was tested and the front of the process, which often determined the quality of the device.

One of the first improvements to the process was to simply install a monitor at the front of the line for the staff to see the test results in real time. This allowed the teams to more easily correlate variation and issues in the process with failures that are found at the end of the line. We also installed testing earlier in the process at the point of first failure and not just at the end of the line after OnStar was fully assembled.

We improved the quality of the OnStar device almost immediately. We achieved higher test yields by allowing the operators to better correlate process parameters such as the amount of solder paste that is needed to improve the soldering of components. The paste is applied very early in the process, and it is no wonder that the staff were not able to improve on the paste operation because they often had no idea of failures at the end of the line where the test was.

Rework was also hidden from those who operate the processes that determine the reliability. The devices that failed the test would be taken off the assembly line and reworked or scrapped, often up to weeks later. This lack of timely feedback as to what caused the failures contributed to not improving. Feedback on what was learned in the rework process was also not shared with the staff in the process step that contributed to the failure.

Healthcare benefits from this same strategy. We always try to give staff at the point of care the ability of inspecting one's own work instead of having someone later in the process inspect and give feedback. An example is in imaging. In the past, a radiographer in a facility might simply take the image only later to hear from the radiologist that it must be retaken because of a lack of precise location or clarity. Now, radiographers have been taught better what the radiologists need in the image, and the imaging equipment makers might also have software that allows immediate image viewing for the radiographers to inspect their own work, while the patient is still positioned for scanning, if needed. With radiation, it is even more critical to *do it right the first time.* Using Deming's principle of *inspect at the source,* healthcare is more able to learn from the past, correct the methods, and lower the number of images that are taken.

We apply Deming's principle in every project. A few other successes in healthcare are the following:

1. *Hand hygiene compliance*—In the past, organizations may have reported their compliance at the end of each month. In *every project,* we report at least daily the compliance within days of chartering at least initially to utilize measurement and management to the measure in real time. Knowing why staff did not practice acceptable hand hygiene at the time of the event makes knowing the root cause easier. This in turn makes finding solutions faster and more effective because we know the root causes. Again and again, we see healthcare organizations throwing someone else's *solution* at the organization's unique set of root causes. In *Utilizing the 3Ms of Process Improvement in Healthcare,* we explore more deeply how we achieve high reliability in hand hygiene and the data collection methods that are now being deployed across the United States and in healthcare facilities in the United Kingdom.

2. *Cardiology teams now know precisely when to transport a patient from his or her preoperative room to the cardiology laboratory by using simple paging devices that are used by restaurants around the globe to tell diners that*

they are ready to be seated. Before, cardiologists might call for the patient an hour or more in advance knowing that the communication between the cardiology laboratory and the inpatient unit often failed resulting in patients not arriving in time.

3. *Blood glucose control is correlated with preventing harm from hospital acquired conditions.* Measuring and managing to the measure a patient's blood glucose levels during surgery instead of hours after surgery helped us reduce infection rates. In one academic medical center, we found that 40% of the procedures encountered blood glucose levels over 200 milligrams/deciliter, realizing the 2014 specification for cardiac surgical patients' level to stay below 180. Measuring levels intraoperatively and post-operatively helps us manage insulin levels soon enough before blood glucose levels exceed tolerances.

Leaders: Empower staff to inspect their work at the source versus relying on inspection that is distant from where and when the quality is determined.

Leaders and engineers: Utilize the 3Ms of process improvement with rounding daily on the measurement of the outcome that is desired and key process measures that mostly drive the outcome.

Reliability Enhanced without Compromise

Working at SKF, a leader in reliability and producer of high-tech products for Formula One race cars, aerospace components, and thousands of other products that keep us safe on the road, air, and water, taught me the importance of achieving zero defects and a practice that they named *scrap without compromise (SWOC)*.

SWOC is simple, hard to swallow initially, and very power-ful in achieving zero defects—a key measure of reliability. The way SWOC works may best be understood using the exam-ple of OnStar's rework at the end of the line. All processes in healthcare and manufacturing, as well as services, have sequential steps. The quality of any step is a function of the steps that precede it. SKF has gotten reliability up at record levels by focusing on the concepts in this book. But, Claes Rehmberg, chief quality officer and my mentor, explained that they still experience some defects escaping to their customers, although rarely.

Claes and others did an in-depth root cause analysis across its sites and found a recurring contributing factor to these defects escaping despite high reliability of the line. A disrup-tion in the flow of the process might result in products or components that are taken offline such as when a failure occurred. The product that was found to vary or to be defec-tive would be taken out of the process. Fine. But, SKF found that any product taken off the line, even if not in the immedi-ate flow of the known defective product, might later contribute to an escaped defect.

The reasons include that part may not experience the same process as if the process was not stopped because it may not reenter the process at the correct assembly step. Or, the product might be inserted back into the flow in the wrong location, and the process applies the wrong identification to the product. The software loads the data elements that are unique to the device incorrectly, and its configuration ends up wrong because the process applies options for the product that preceded it.

Similarly, in surgery, we have seen the wrong image dis-played. This could have been because the sequence of the operating room (OR) schedule changed, and the image dis-played in the OR for the surgical team is that of the patient that was on the table previously.

Disrupting and adding complexity to a process similar to healthcare organizations that recognize disruptions in preparing medicines for inpatients can be dangerous because the person preparing the medicines may not complete all the steps or duplicate the steps, which can cause medical errors. These organizations have supplied vests that remind others to not disturb or have provided quieter, less congested areas to minimize disruptions resulting in medical errors.

Even with more real-time measurement and improvement in the OnStar device, we still had a few failures at the customer's assembly plant. High-reliability organizations take a system approach to achieve reliability. In the manufacturing process, the wake-up feature worked. However, some OnStar devices that passed in our facility failed at the vehicle assembly plant.

Leaders: Ask how each person's tasks may affect others in the system. Drive mindfulness of the system, not just the process in isolation.

This latter cause is what we found with the OnStar product. Each OnStar device has a unique identification. This identification is critical to ensure that the telematics device wakes up and can communicate in the cellular network. We found the wrong ID in the devices that were returned from the assembly plant and traced it back to a disruption in the manufacturing process and loading the data elements into the wrong OnStar device. We should have scrapped the devices in and around the disruption, as SKF learned years earlier. Saving a unit or two was not worth the costs and loss of credibility in the reliability of OnStar.

We implemented the SWOC with the other improvements and achieved high reliability for which Motorola is well known. After all, Six Sigma was developed by Motorola to achieve the high reliability that is still known today in its first responder radios, which are used in most healthcare organizations where reliability is critical.

Probability Measures in Reliability

A Mathematical Definition of Reliability

$$R(t) = \Pr\{T > t\} = \int_{t}^{\infty} f(x)\,dx$$

Where $f(x)$ is the probability of failure density function, and t is the length of the period of time (which is assumed to start from time zero).

The key in this mathematical definition is the following:

■ The intended function must be clearly defined with a system in mind. Despite zero defects among the system components, failure may still occur in the system because of interactions between system components. The intended function must be stated as a system for its components and interactions to be properly designed. Deming's Profound Knowledge and its focus on the system are apparent again. The requirements of reliability must be a system requirement. A healthcare example is in treating sepsis after identifying its risk. The time to first fluid bolus and time to first antibiotic may mean the difference between survival and death. The system of care in the emergency department (ED) is very different from the system for a direct admission to a medical/surgical unit. The ED may have processes that are designed for earlier identification and starting the first fluid bolus than in a very busy inpatient floor. In fact, we found this to be true and had to redesign the inpatient unit system to get an earlier admission assessment and a quicker preparation for starting fluids and antibiotics.

■ Specified time between failures must be stated. The variable *t* refers to the specified period of time that the intended function is expected to perform. Accelerated life testing, when a function is cycled more quickly than expected in actual application, is valuable in designing products and services before they are sold.

■ Parameters need to be stated in a complete defnition of reliability. No product or service is expected to survive in harsher conditions than intended in the design. An example is a surgical site closure technique for a total hip replacement for a patient who begins therapy earlier than intended and too aggressively.

There are different equations in reliability because the formulae are based on the type of data and the purpose of the reliability analysis. In addition to the equation to calculate the reliability of an outcome, there are other characteristics in measuring reliability that we need to appreciate.

Reliability analysis is often more complex than other experimental analyses because some experiments include knowledge of the outcome of every entity in the experiment. An example is when we study the readmission rates of 2000 patients, and our experimental data account for the entire 2000 patients through a 30-day postdischarge period of concern. We have the outcome of all 2000 patients and thus can predict the reliability using the probability of failure. What if we only track through 30 days, as is the custom in healthcare, yet we want to understand the probability of readmission regardless of when the readmission occurs because that is how the patient will measure reliability?

Data Characteristics in Reliability Analysis

Reliability, as we know, is measuring how well the requirements are met through time. Healthcare leaders and engineers need to understand how the reliability formulae take into account what is known, and unknown, in stating reliability.

Exact Time or Interval Time Data

Surgical site infections and readmissions work provide healthcare examples of the complexity of reliability analysis. Let us say that we are interested in knowing the reliability of infection-free surgery. Due to CMS rules, healthcare is often considered a success if no condition occurs within 30 days of discharge. We study 1000 patients and consider a failure to be any patient who acquired an infection between the time of surgery and 30 days after the date of the procedure in this example. We could monitor the exact time or interval to record any infections, i.e., failure. An exact-time type of data might be obtained by checking for an infection every day. If we find an infection, we record the date that we first discover it. This is called exact time.

Often, healthcare batches observations, which does not allow us to know the exact time. Surgical patients are often scheduled to see their primary care physician (PCP) in seven days after discharge. If an infection is found at the PCP appointment, we do not know the exact date that the infection occurred. We can only state the infection as occurring in the interval between discharge and seven days later. This is an example of interval time data. Interval time data are less precise than exact time data but may be the only data that we can get.

Censored Data

Censored data are another dimension in reliability analysis that we have to understand so that we do not make incorrect decisions on how reliable our outcomes are, such as in understanding how reliable we are in preventing hospital-acquired conditions and readmissions.

Knowing what we do not know is critical in becoming a high-reliability organization.

We do not know about infections past the 30 days. We call this censored data. Censored data is data when we don't know the exact time of failure. Studying infections after a surgical procedure often includes censored data.

We can plot the patients who acquired an infection within the 30-day time period, but we cannot plot the infection of any patient after the 30 days because we stopped collecting data at 30 days. The right tail of the distribution of the time of infection, therefore, is unknown. This is called censored data. It is right censored, to be more descriptive. It is critical in calculating the reliability to know if we have censored data and what their type is. Left-censored data are common when we have infections before we start looking and then start observing and recording the exact time or interval. We do not know the times in the left tail of the distribution.

I have now covered three of the more important characteristics in data collection and analysis in understanding how reliable healthcare outcomes and processes are. With this information, my intention is for leaders and engineers to understand the uniqueness of data collection in reliability analysis. I think that understanding the exact time or interval time, censoring, and how multiple failure modes can be discovered reinforces better data collection. For more details on reliability formulae for most of the data healthcare will need, see the reliability engineering book listed with the references at the end of this chapter.

Failure Modes

Reliability analysis in healthcare often has to account for multiple failure modes. The number of ways a patient's healing can fail are another validation that healthcare is complex.

CMS recently announced that it proposes to reinforce higher reliability in the highest-volume surgical procedures in the United States—total knee or hip replacements. At present, CMS considers patients who are readmitted within 30 days of discharge a failure in its excess readmission penalty program. The proposal is to consider select readmissions as failures through 90 days. I will look at readmissions throughout 90 days, not just 30 days after the original admission as it has done. Our work shows that readmissions often follow a multimodal distribution shape. We look for a change in the rate of readmissions after admission, procedure, or discharge beyond the 30 days to have a more robust healthcare treatment plan and better reliability. Just looking within CMS 30-day period illustrates that readmissions often follow a multimodal distribution, which may point to different reasons for the readmissions. If we only look at the 30-day period as a whole, we make our work to discover the root causes more difficult than if we look at exact times. (Again, exact times are more helpful than interval times.)

To understand a multimodal distribution, please look at Figure 2.1, which is a dot plot of the count of patients who are readmitted from a fairly stable daily population of knee and hip replacements. Each dot represents a patient who was readmitted and the days that elapsed from admission to the date of readmission. Let us focus on the patients who received a knee replacement.

There are hundreds of potential reasons and combinations of factors that can lead to readmissions. A patient might need to be readmitted due to complications from poor nutrition, not taking medicines, or overaggressive therapy. Each of these

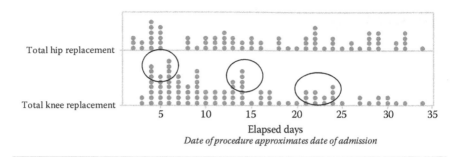

Figure 2.1   Dot plot of days until readmission for knee and hip replacement.

reasons might be represented by a mode or peak in the failure rate or a simple count of patients who are readmitted using a dot plot.

Plotting when the readmission occurs relative to the admission date may help us find the root cause of the readmission. Overaggressive therapy too early in rehabilitation might be seen very early after discharge. Wound dehiscence is an all-too-common reason for readmission. Dehiscence is when there is a parting of the layers of a surgical wound. Either the surface layers separate or the whole wound splits open. This can be caused by a number of factors including overaggressive therapy, not having prophylactic antibiotics before or after surgery allowing infections, and sutures that open.

Not taking medicines might result in a readmission that is represented in the right tail of the distribution of all the patients returning. The patients may stop taking medicines too soon, especially antibiotics to prevent infection, because they are feeling fine. Another unfortunate reason is that they do not have enough money to pay for the medicines. This situation often occurs soon after the medicines given to the patient during the hospital stay run out.

Poor nutrition might result in a surgical site infection, which may not manifest itself until 20–30 days, but poor nutrition could result in a readmission much faster in comorbidity situations such as a patient with diabetes and other disorders where nutrition deficiency exacerbates conditions.

Reliability analysis may need to be complex in complex healthcare processes. Oversimplifying methods gains nothing.

References

1. Tobias, P. A. and Trindade, D. C. 2012. *Applied Reliability, Third Edition.* Boca Raton, FL, Taylor & Francis Group.
2. CHRISTUS Santa Rosa. 2015. *National Patient Safety Foundation 17th Annual National Patient Safety Congress.* Austin, TX, April 29–May 1, 2015.

Chapter 3

Leadership Principles in High-Reliability Organizations

Introduction

Knowing that reliability is getting the expected outcome throughout the expected time, high-reliability organizations (HROs) can be simply defined as organizations that achieve reliability.

I spent more than 20 years learning about and improving reliability at Cutler-Hammer, an Eaton Corporation business and a leader in electrical safety products. Cutler-Hammer has been making power distribution products for over 100 years and is considered one of the highest-quality manufacturers in the United States.* Customers who bought our products

---

* The United States' largest home builder, David Weekley Homes, again recognized Eaton Cutler-Hammer with its top quality and service award. "Each year we recognize those best-of-breed companies that provide an optimum combination of quality and service, according to the results of our rigorous evaluation process. Our goal in using this evaluation and feedback platform is to ensure Our Homebuyers and Homeowners receive a world-class home buying experience from the entire Team, including our trading partners." Available at http://www.davidweekleyhomes.com/page/partners-of-choice-awards.

wanted the products to distribute electricity safely and efficiently.

My next company was SKF, where I led Quality for the U.S. Seals Division. This company shifted its entire focus from making buggy whips for horse-drawn carriage drivers to making a more reliable way to keep grease on the axle for Henry Ford's alternative to horses. Henry came to the founders looking for a way to seal in grease that is critical for the reliability of the car axle.

Working for Motorola with General Motors (GM) and Bayerische Motoren Werke AG (BMW) as customers, we made driving safer and more reliable by alerting emergency care providers in times of passenger danger. The technology was named OnStar and BMW Assist and, even though safety was on the minds of GM and BMW for their customers, they bought products and technology, not safety.

Today, I apply these same methods that made Eaton, SKF, and Motorola providers of some of the world's most reliable projects and services. At United Airlines, my team developed and launched its Lean Six Sigma and again applied the concepts in flight operations to improve safety in the cabin for an already top safety aviation carrier. I learned more from United Airlines in how to achieve safety than I gave. How reliable is United Airlines in safety? They have not had a fatality since 1978 caused by human error. Their culture of safety is everything that we talk about in healthcare such as the work from Reason, Weick, and Sutcliffe, which will be covered in this book.

In more recent times, healthcare clients are now utilizing these methods including the leadership principles to become better leaders or to improve performance in caring for patients.

Cutler-Hammer's products most familiar to consumers are circuit breakers in homes and power panels for campsites. Considering those who talk about high reliability in terms of aerospace, I add that Eaton was chosen by NASA to provide a key component in the automatic landing system of the Space Shuttle and components for the B-1 Bomber.

Reliability Begins with Design

Cutler-Hammer's customers for the product built in the factory I managed included electrical distributors, electricians, do-it-yourself centers such as Home Depot, and home and business owners. Every one of our customers purchased these products to be a component of a larger electrical distribution system distributing power safely. My favorite product was a combination circuit breaker box and electrical meter named "Power Outlet Panel." I am most proud of it because it was developed with our customers and the process to make it was designed with our frontline staff who were going to produce and assemble the devices in Lincoln, IL. The people who bought these products were recreational vehicle park owners or electricians. They installed our products for people who camped to allow them safe access to electricity. They wanted the outcome of power to their campsite. Do not get me wrong that safety is not important to our customers. We think that we sold a lot of these power panels because park owners found our panels to be safer than our competitors' and may have been the key criteria to buy our panels, but their primary purpose in purchasing was to distribute power safely all of the time for the expected lifetime of the device or application.

Hill Country Memorial Hospital— Leadership and Reliability

The Malcolm Baldrige Quality Award recognizes leaders in quality and reliability. Healthcare has been increasing engagement with the process over the years since Motorola was one of the first recipients of the award. In 2014, Hill Country Memorial (HCM), an acute care hospital in Fredericksburg, TX, won the award. The following is an interview with Jayne E. Pope, its chief executive officer; Debbye Wallace-Dooley, executive director, business intelligence; and Vicki Audette, communications strategist.* And, I cannot leave out team members who greet everyone at the front desk and were warm and inviting. They exemplified high reliability in their treatment of those who enter who are often concerned and anxious. I think that their story has valuable lessons in helping healthcare achieve high reliability. HCM, as you will see, has achieved higher reliability than most of the nation's acute care hospitals in many ways.

First of all, their patients score HCM as one of the best in the nation on the likelihood to recommend a question. Fred Reichheld, in his book, *The Ultimate Question* (2011), shares that scoring high in this question shows high loyalty among an organization's customers, and higher margins correlate with loyalty. See Figures 3.1 and 3.2.

The likelihood to recommend question is an important measure both in terms of comparing hospitals and in the providers' willingness to recommend because just one surgeon can impact the revenue and margins significantly. Jayne believes in empowering staff in gathering the voice of the patients and families, and my first impression walking in the door confirmed that her staff are dedicated to listening and assisting anyone who walks in the door. I was met by the volunteer at the reception desk who guessed that I was the person coming to interview them for the book and greeted me by name. I am still not sure how she knew this. That is the magic of HCM and its focus on others.

Perhaps, this ultimate question is another reason for healthcare organizations that struggle financially to improve reliability as Jayne and her team have done.

---

* Interview with Jayne Pope, CEO Hill Country Memorial in Fredericksburg, TX, and executive staff. February 2, 2015.

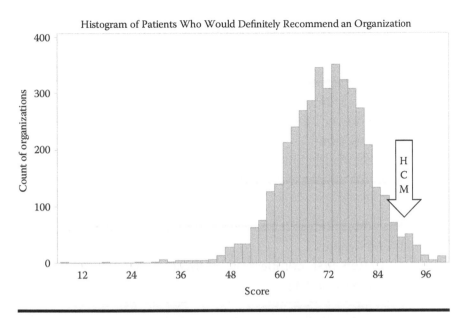

Figure 3.1   National distribution of percentage of top-box responses by organization (CMS Provider ID). (From Hospital Compare, July 2013–June 2014.)

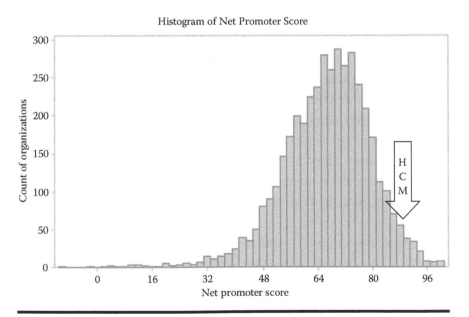

Figure 3.2   Distribution of national Net Promoter Score. (From Hospital Compare, July 2013–June 2014.)

Jayne began with the most succinct, telling, and interesting vision, mission, and values statements.

HCM's vision:
　　Empower others. Create healthy.
Their mission:
　　Remarkable always.

HCM's values:
　　Others first, compassion, innovation, accountability, stewardship

---

■ *Empower others.* Just today, I saw in a hospital about the size of HCM a group of managers and executives who were trying really hard to improve the outcomes. They went from one meeting to the next—three consecutive meetings virtually back to back. Yet, this site's history is a lot of ideas that were tried and are still ranking below the national median in every patient experience composite score. In an HRO like HCM, we see empowered frontline staff taking responsibility to serve the patients and their colleagues in small team problem-solving activities in the workplace. They know what the outcome measures mean and what their current performance level is and realize that the entire world can see via HCM's website.

HCM shares its goals and measures publicly including the names of the people who were responsible for the goals and improvements. If that is not transparent enough, they invite former patients to provide even more feedback. And, they share the results of these polls on their website. No one hides issues in an HRO. No one feels the need to do that because

an HRO has a just culture, an empowered staff, and a leadership leading change. These attributes reinforce continuous
improvement.

What I saw today at this other hospital were frustrated
managers—frustrated because they try so hard and yet still
cannot get everything done. At the same time, not one frontline staff could explain what the charts meant on their shiny
new performance boards that were posted on each unit a
distant six months ago. The managers were frustrated when
they found that the noise-level devices to help patients rest
were turned off. My simple questions were the following: Who
from the frontline staff were involved in the effort to learn
why patients rate the hospital lower than the national median?
Who from the frontline staff decided to purchase the noise-
level devices? Who decided where to put them? Who would
be responsible to monitor the devices to see if they have an
effect? There were no answers, because not even the frontline
supervisors were part of the change. Another idea was tried
by someone else with a lot of honest efforts to improve yet
nothing to show for it except energy that was spent with no
result.

- *Compassion.* Hill Country has a strategy that where
  administration, staff, and providers are aligned with their
  patients' values. They recruit based on this value. In case
  you are thinking that Hill Country has all employed physicians, they do not. Hill Country has some physicians that
  are employed, but the majority are not. The physicians
  are partners in a small community that is surrounded by
  San Antonio, Austin, and towns that are in-between the
  size of these cities and Fredericksburg, TX.

Baldrige examiners tested how well HCM's values are
shared among the physicians. They asked three focus groups
of physicians. The examiners saw firsthand the pride that the
physicians had in HCM and the physicians' knowledge of the

values. Physician engagement at these high levels must surely be a contributor in HCM receiving one of the highest scores in the likelihood to recommend HCM to friends and family. The leadership team stated that the physicians should go on working with the HCM staff for continuous improvement.

Learning is not just for the frontline staff. The Chief Operating Officer (COO) is trained in the Toyota Production System, and HCM also invested having staff trained in performance improvement.

Training staff in performance improvement is a struggle for many. HCM, too, initially struggled with some training. Jayne mentioned that they have tried many things and certainly did not have success using classroom training. They found that walking people through plan–do–check–act (PDCA) made sense. So, they introduced PDCA with quarterly coaching plans. Each department has an alignment board to show cascaded goals from the vision, mission, and values.

Jayne also believes in empowering patients and making them a partner in their care versus *doing healthcare to them*.

Strategy is one of the seven elements, and Hill Country shares its strategy on the World Wide Web to include everyone. Frontline staff participate in strategy mapping and thus communicate the strategy better than those who talk about strategy at an annual meeting. Check out their strategy map at http://www.hillcountrymemorial.org/page/about-hcm/strategy-map/.

Building relationships is a core competency, according to Jayne. Two of Hill Country's highest strengths are processes of care and patient experience measures using CMS' value-based purchasing's measures as evidence. Living the values card can be a patient story, and it gets to the management chain.

■ *Create healthy.* HROs focus on preventing problems, even if it cuts into their revenue. Sacrificing quality and reliability below customer expectations is a failure that is due to occur. Create healthy makes it more imperative to decrease errors and makes sure that people are healthy.

They know that financial performance is key in achieving the mission. They, therefore, have a healthy balance sheet and work to support the community with its gala event and make it easy for the community to know HCM and participate in its operations. It is remarkable for such a small town to have invested in a wellness center. Fredericksburg is also fairly remote from competition. However, outside markets created a need to change to focus on what was the more immediate need of the surrounding communities.

An interesting and humorous story is when Baldrige asked for examples of dissatisfaction. Jayne and the team struggled to show the breakout of the distribution because they had only favorable results using the prescribed measurement. Jayne reported a great job of developing a plan, but executing and deploying were key. Staff members have goals that support the balanced scorecard that everyone can see on their website. They manage to the measure with quarterly coaching plans with staff.

Strategic breakthrough initiatives have war rooms to cover the quarter's results and to ensure that even the frontline staff know what is important and the current and past performance. A weekly report is also conducted to manage to the measure and recognize people for contributing.

Physicians have a care oversight committee. They own responsibility for the quality of care that is provided. Physicians peer-review and take it very seriously. Surgeons wanted to participate in NSQIP, a system from the American College of Surgeons, which includes data and benchmarking to improve the reliability of surgery.*

HCM continues in its quest for higher reliability and as a recipient of the Malcolm Baldrige Award, as Motorola has achieved twice, Jayne and her team agreed to share what they

---

* American College of Surgeons' National Surgical Quality Improvement Program® (ACS NSQIP®). ACS NSQIP is the leading nationally validated, risk-adjusted, outcome-based program to measure and improve the quality of surgical care in the private sector.

have learned and how they achieved higher quality and reliability for all those who seek them out.

Lastly, the leadership team believes that high reliability improves their revenue. Jayne mentioned that the foundation raised over $3 million as a case in point. High reliability also reduces the costs that are spent on failures and referrals that are going elsewhere. Leading in quality and reliability pays, not costs, an organization.

Chapter 4

The Culture of High-Reliability Organizations

The Culture of Safety and Its Subcultures

The works of Karl Weick, Kathleen Sutcliffe, and James Reason are popular in healthcare safety practices. I united their thoughts into one diagram.[1,2] In their books on reliability in safety, they share similar concepts of the subcultures making up a culture where safety is achieved. In no way are these a dichotomy as you see the comparison that is diagrammed in Table 4.1.

Weick and Sutcliffe, in their book *Managing the Unexpected: Resilient Performance in an Age of Uncertainty* (2007), break a safety culture into five subcultures. Reason, in his book *Managing the Risks of Organizational Accidents* (1997), also has five subcultures. Essentially, both authors' concepts match well with Reason's just culture leading the cultures.

A just culture is a prerequisite to Reason's other four subcultures. His point is that people must feel that they will be treated fairly, justly, if they report, which is Reason's second subculture. It might be considered a bit masochistic if people

Table 4.1 Subcultures in a Safety Culture Compared

	Connecting a Safety Culture with Mindfulness in High-Reliability Organizations				
	1. Just Culture	**2. Reporting Culture**	**3. Learning Culture**	**4. Informed Culture**	**5. Flexible Culture**
Subcultures in a Safety Culture (Reason)	People know what is acceptable and are reinforced to report accidents and close calls.	An organizational climate in which people are prepared to report their errors and close calls.	A willingness and competence to draw the right conclusions and the will to implement major reforms.	Those who manage and operate the system have current knowledge about the process and variation.	Ability to reconfigure in the face of high-tempo operations or certain kinds of danger.
Mindfulness to Prevent Accidents (Weick, Sutcliffe)		*Deference to expertise* Supervisors listen and respond to the staff.	*Reluctance to simplify* Avoiding overly simple explanations of failure.	*Preoccupation with failure* Close calls are viewed as evidence of systems that should be improved to reduce potential harm. *Sensitivity to operations* Constant awareness by leaders and staff of the state of the systems.	*Resilience* Leaders and staff who are trained and prepared to know how to respond when system failures do occur.

report in a culture where they know that they will be unjustly treated, for example, terminated, if they report a safety issue.

Reason believes that a just culture leads to a reporting culture, which then allows a culture of learning. In aviation, virtually every accident is publicly reported with the intention that other pilots will learn from accidents and make aviation safer. A learning culture leads to an informed culture where defects are caught in real time to prevent failure. Lastly, a culture needs to be flexible to adjust to the reality of a quickly progressing sequence of events with variation ever present.

Weick and Sutcliffe equate a culture of safety as one of mindfulness. It is a deference to expertise where leaders and supervisors respect those frontline caregivers who know how the care processes really work and thus have insights into what to do when safety is at risk. Reason's subculture of a reporting culture and flexible culture recognize the value of the frontline staff and empowers them to act. Table 4.1 continues the detail of each subculture and how Reason's work mates with Weick and Sutcliffe's.

Leaders: Own the maturing of the organization in these cultures to achieve high-reliability.

Engineers: Own the reduction in risks and reduce them quickly because building these subcultures does not happen overnight. Having unreliable processes without a mature culture of safety and mindfulness is double trouble.

The Agency for Healthcare Research and Quality (AHRQ) in 2008 sponsored work in how healthcare organizations should become high-reliability organizations (HROs).[3] They, too, pulled from the work of Reason and Weick and Sutcliffe in developing the flow of achieving the *ultimate outcome* of exceptionally safe, consistently high-quality care. See Figure 4.1.

There is no definitive line of demarcation between organizations that are considered by some to be HROs and those that are not. There also have been organizations that were considered to be HROs and now would be considered not so reliable. Even HROs have mishaps, and using the definition of reliability, some organizations have achieved the expected outcomes for an expected period of time, true. An example is an ambulatory surgical center that has had no falls, wrong-site surgeries, *sticks* (a stick is an unintended breaking of the skin by a needle), sharp injury, retained foreign objects, or other patient or staff mishaps for a year. However, if one looks deep enough, there will have been close calls that some may consider unacceptable for an HRO. I know of no organization that is completely reliable in everything that it does despite

Specific considerations	General orientation	Impact on processes	Ultimate outcome
Sensitivity to operations			
Preoccupation with failure			
Deference to expertise	State of mindfulness	High reliability	Exceptionally safe, consistently high-quality care
Resilience			
Reluctance to simplify			

Figure 4.1   The five specific concepts that help create the state of mindfulness needed for reliability, which in turn is a prerequisite for safety. (From Hines, S. et al., *Becoming a High-Reliability Organization: Operational Advice for Hospital Leaders.* **[Prepared by the Lewin Group under Contract No. 290-04-0011.] AHRQ Publication No. 08-0022, Rockville, MD: Agency for Healthcare Research and Quality, 2008.)**

anything that happens to its environment. Zero defects is not a requirement of being an HRO, so what differentiates HROs from others?

Principles Common among HROs

The following material is taken from my books *Utilizing the 3Ms of Process Improvement* and *Utilizing the 3Ms of Process Improvement in Healthcare* (2012).

Weick and Sutcliffe believe that HROs are mindful of variation occurring and ways that failures occur and thus are more able to prevent accidents than those who are not mindful. They found five elements to being mindful. They are the following:

1. *Sensitivity to operations.* Preserving constant awareness by leaders and staff of the state of the systems and processes that affect patient care. This awareness is key to noting risks and preventing them.
2. *Reluctance to simplify.* Simple processes are good, but simplistic explanations for why things work or fail are risky. Avoiding overly simple explanations of failure (unqualified staff, inadequate training, communication failure, etc.) is essential in order to understand the true reasons why people are placed at risk.
3. *Preoccupation with failure.* When near misses occur, these are viewed as evidence of systems that should be improved to reduce potential harm to patients. Rather than viewing near hits as proof that the system has effective safeguards, they are viewed as symptomatic of areas that are in need of more attention.
4. *Deference to expertise.* If leaders and supervisors are not willing to listen and respond to the insights of staff who know how processes really work and the risks that

patients really face, you will not have a culture in which high-reliability is possible.

5. *Resilience.* Leaders and staff need to be trained and prepared to know how to respond when system failures do occur.

Adding to the discussion of HROs, I found the work of Carolyn Libuser helpful in identifying the elements of HROs.[4] She lists five elements, and one will see some of Weick and Sutcliffe's concepts. I will share actual healthcare examples within each of her elements and cross her ideas with mine and Weick and Sutcliffe's.

The Elements of an HRO

1. *Process auditing.* Processes shift, and one must know early when such shifting is beginning, take action when the shifting warrants, and learn and act to make the process more robust. Leaders, process auditing is your responsibility. If done well, leaders are out in the processes and among the staff performing the work within the cycles of expected vacation. Engineers, your role in process auditing is to help leaders know what processes to audit, what to look for, and when to audit. When to audit is called process audit cycles. The expected cycles of variation are your responsibility. If designed well, engineers have performed tests that help determine failure modes and the variables that are involved in these failure modes. And, the engineers have measured the reliability of the process using one of the measures of reliability such as the mean time between failures. The time between failures helps determine the time of the cycles of failure, which aids in determining what to audit and how frequently (the cycle) to audit. And yes, random audits are important to understand how the process is normally

operating. One type of variation, by definition, is random, and leaders will better sample the process when auditing is random within the cycles of performance.

An example of process auditing occurs daily in clinical care in the discharge process. A hospital found that its patients' average length of stay (LOS) was longer than the Centers for Medicare & Medicaid (CMS) averages. No, the hospital was not just trying to reduce the unreimbursed cost. CMS reimbursement may not cover the actual LOS, but the hospital chose to manage its LOS to best prepare the patients for discharge and not expose them to additional risks, such as acquiring an infection during the stay.

The process audits were specifically timed around the end of the week and beginning of the week because a variable found in the improvement work was extended LOS because providers were less likely to discharge on the weekends. A patient not discharged on Friday had a statistically significant longer LOS considering all other factors. Leaders audited the discharge process on Fridays and through Mondays to pick up any deviation in the clinical care that could extend the LOS over the weekend.

2. *Appropriate reward system.* Fundamental to reliability is rewarding reliability. Thus, it makes sense that leaders reward behaviors supporting reliability and coach in the moment behaviors, which occur counter to reliability. Auditing the process facilitates this element because leaders are among the people performing the processes and seeing the behaviors firsthand. An example of rewarding the right behavior at the right time occurred at CHRISTUS Santa Rosa Medical Center by Chris Bowe, president of the acute care hospital. Chris was auditing the new inventory management replenishment process out in place to improve the reliability of minimizing the time under anesthesia during surgery. The team found that too often, surgical staff did not have the sterile supplies that are needed at the time of surgery, and they needed to exit the operating

room to locate missing supplies. Exiting the surgical room can delay the case and thus prolong the time that the patient is under anesthesia. This time should be minimized to reduce complications and risks to the patient.

The major root cause of the supply shortage was a late replenishment. The replenishment was delayed because the materials staff were not aware that the supplies were out. The most common cause of unreliable inventory status systems is the need for humans to tell the computer what they consumed and the computer to be set for constant inventory updates. Kanban, a pull system based on consumption, was implemented because it is very easy to know when supplies run low, and it is a simple and reliable system that is used by Toyota and every company where I worked. Kanban often allows more reliable replenishment just in time because it is simpler than some systems that are too reliant on humans interfacing well with computer replenishment and financial charging systems. The most beautiful outcome of this process was how Chris recognized Anna Marie, Stacy, and the entire surgical and materials staff members as he walked the surgical floor in his audits.

Leaders of HROs round frequently, and rewarding the right behaviors is a characteristic that many staff share when asked how their leaders act toward them.

3. *Avoiding quality degradation.* Letting things slip is not what makes reliability happen. Referring to the Kanban system, the team immediately takes action when a Kanban is not turned in when supplies run low. If a team member sees a Kanban in a bin that should have been turned in, the member will turn it in and notify the team. In organizations that struggle with Kanban, often, it is this failure mode of not turning in Kanbans and running out of supplies. This causes others to lose confidence in this simple system and may eventually destroy the benefits altogether.

Another example of quality degradation is blood glucose control in patients who have undergone coronary artery bypass graft surgery. Evidence-based care proves that the risk of infection is lower if blood glucose is well managed, which is to keep the glucose levels under 180 and not too low to cause hypoglycemia. Once the blood glucose levels near either boundary, treatment should occur quickly because further degradation could be life threatening. That is why hourly checks and protocols that are sensitive to the variation in levels are important to prevent catastrophic degradation.

4. *Risk perception.* Weick and Sutcliffe call this sensitivity to operations. Perception of risk through constant awareness, as Weick and Sutcliffe state, prevents quality degradation, is often initiated by process auditing, and is learned by rewarding risk mindfulness. Team strategies and tools to enhance performance and patient safety (TeamSTEPPS) is a powerfully effective program to reduce risks by rewarding risk perception and taking action. As a master and trainer in TeamSTEPPS, I learned how to recognize when people perceive risk and to help organizations change behaviors to perceive risk and act.

TeamSTEPPS was developed by the AHRQ and the U.S. Department of Defense. TeamSTEPPS is an evidence-based program that is aimed at optimizing performance among teams of healthcare professionals—enabling them to respond quickly and effectively to whatever situations arise. Teamwork has been found to be one of the key initiatives within patient safety that can transform the culture. Communication is key in achieving reliability because early perception of risk allows further degradation of quality. Speaking up when risk is perceived is the right and responsibility of everyone in an HRO. Libuser uses the term command control in a way that highlights the accountability more than power. I would use the term single-point accountability because the author recognizes that organizations need to be clear about where decisions need to be made at any point in time and circumstance.

TeamSTEPPS provides the education for leaders and all staff in how to speak up when risk is perceived.

Leaders: If you have not considered TeamSTEPPS in your quest for higher reliability, let me make it easier for you with a link to the AHRQ website: http://www.ahrq.gov.

- *Migrating decision making.* Reason, Weick, and Sutcliffe all agree that decision making in times of risk is benefitted by those on the front line who have better knowledge of the situation. Deference to expertise is the term that Weick and Sutcliffe share.
- *Redundancy of people or hardware.* Even HROs have failure. Engineers, take note. It is not a sign of weakness to suggest redundancy in your beautiful new creation if the existing technology is not reliable. In this example of information technology (IT) in healthcare, redundancy is needed. How many times have you heard or witnessed the frustration of a clinician while charting and the system is slow or goes down completely? What if the computerized autopilot failed, as it has, in the aircraft halfway across the Pacific Ocean? What if the hydraulic brake system in the school bus fails? What if the oxygen line in an intensive care unit fails? Accidents can happen, even in well-designed systems, and reliability engineers predict the possibility and have backups, redundancy, or options to maintain performance if failure of the primary system occurs.
- *Senior managers with "the big picture."* Libuser focuses again on leadership's critical role in achieving reliability. Perhaps it is time to acknowledge the all-too-common

failure of promoting great frontline staff into management without supporting the staff with management and leadership training. Who has not seen an excellent-performing nurse or physician later struggle in a management role? Why is this so common? Let us go back to the person's college years.

There were tracks and degrees for professions such as nursing, biology, chemistry, IT, and industrial engineering. Business administration, sociology, psychology, and fine arts are found, as well, in most colleges and universities. I thought that chemistry was interesting and went to my first university counseling session ready to sign up for chemistry classes, only to be lured into a new engineering program titled energy physics. To make the long story short, I ended my first degree in business administration, which may seem like quite a change from chemistry or physics.

The reasons are twofold. One, I liked the more general and broader studies more than concentration within physics and the science classes in the physics degree program. And two, I loved music and found that running the business of a band was really fun. A degree in business did not require time at night in labs like science did.

To be successful in a musical performance, especially by not being the best drummer on Earth, one needs to be able to see the big picture of entertainment and manage hundreds of variables. I liked everything about the business from managing the road crew and sound engineer, working with agencies and venue owners, the marketing and promotion, capital equipment design and sourcing (we found higher profits by investing in larger sound systems and light shows), and most of all, entertaining. There is instant gratification and feedback when a business owner stays in touch with the customers. Staying close to customers and what they value helps focus on the big picture. This closeness of leadership to the patients in healthcare is one of the most beneficial facets of leading healthcare.

At Motorola, United Airlines, and even The Joint Commission, it takes extra energy for executives and directors to literally interface with the customers. With United, when we did not go out to the terminals or fly, or at Eaton Electrical, if we did not go to job sites while our equipment was being installed, we often lost the big picture and wasted energy on the minutiae that did not matter as much to the people who are availing our services.

- *Formal rules and procedures.* Ignorance of the law, especially in physics, kills. I enjoyed a fictional work, *The Martian* (2014), by Andy Weir.[5] Here is an excerpt and a lesson when ignorance of the law is dangerous:
- "But physical law is a pushy little ..., and it exacted revenge for the additional weight. I only got 57 kilometers before I was out of juice" (p. 434). This excerpt is about the astronaut who got stranded on Mars, preparing to trek across Mars to be rescued.

Science is wonderful because it knows what it knows and everything else that a scientist knows not to assume. The astronaut survives through the first half of the book, at least, despite the dangers surrounding him. He survives because he knows and complies with the laws of physics and chemistry and the procedures that NASA developed to reduce risks. When he breaks those laws or procedures, something bad usually happens. NASA broke with the procedure in circumventing preflight testing and lost an entire craft that is destined to Mars for rescuing the astronaut.

The protocol often broken in surgery is the Universal Protocol. This protocol requires the entire surgical team to stop and verify the site, side, and procedure prior to entry. In every wrong-site surgery I investigated, this protocol was broken. Libuser is correct; formal rules and procedures, when correct for the situation, increase reliability.

■ *Training.* I am thankful that Libuser included training and that she listed it last. Last is important because healthcare loves to suggest that training, or retraining, is all that is needed. As I write on my iPad, I have no troubles writing this book without any training that is specific to this device whatsoever. Training is necessary when complexity and lack of experience exist. Healthcare is complex, and training is critical.

If an organization truly designs for high-reliability, training will be a part of the design. The training will be simplified for easier capture. The ability of the staff will be audited, tested, and rewarded. Their knowledge will be tested on quality and risks, how to mitigate risks, and continuous improvement with the big picture in mind, and students will know the rules and procedures well.

References

1. Weick, K. E. and Sutcliffe, K. M. 2007. *Managing the Unexpected: Resilient Performance in an Age of Uncertainty.* New York: Wiley.
2. Reason, J. 1997. *Managing the Risks of Organizational Accidents.* Surrey, UK: Ashgate.
3. Hines, S., Luna, K., Lofthus, J. et al. 2008. *Becoming a High-Reliability Organization: Operational Advice for Hospital Leaders.* (Prepared by the Lewin Group under Contract No. 290-04-0011.) AHRQ Publication No. 08-0022. Rockville, MD: Agency for Healthcare Research and Quality.
4. Libuser, C. B. 1994. *Organization Structure and Risk Mitigation.* Dissertation submitted in partial satisfaction of the requirements for the degree of Doctor of Philosophy in Management. Los Angeles: University of California.
5. Weir, A. 2014. Excerpt from *The Martian.* New York: Broadway Books, iBooks.

Chapter 5

Management Principles in Reliability

Practice Makes More Reliable

High-reliability organizations (HROs) practice failing. They have a process in identifying risks, prioritizing them, and then practicing what to do when they occur. Libuser[1] found that financial institutions that achieve higher reliability also audit processes. Auditing processes adds to the knowledge of risk and is a conduit to leadership about behaviors that are accompanied with data that are checks on the quality and reliability of the processes that result in the outcomes. Dr. Deming helped us understand the difference between inspection and auditing.

What many confuse to be auditing is really inspecting—and it is disrespectful to the front line and a waste of leadership time. In leading HROs, every level of management knows its roles and responsibilities in achieving high reliability including inspection and auditing. Leaders audit the processes leaving the frontline to inspect during the work. Inspecting should be a part of the frontline's normal work and only as necessary to assure quality and safety. Leadership defers this in-process inspection to the experts—the frontline who should have everything they need to know what is needed. The frontline and real-time mindfulness to the process allows early discovery of variation as it begins to occur. Engineering a process for reliability may include statistical process control charting, which aids the frontline in discovering variation so they can take action to prevent failure. We share more of these techniques throughout the book. Dynamic discovery is critical in achieving high reliability. Steven Spear, in his book *Chasing the Rabbit* (2009),[2] coined the term dynamic discovery, referring to the constant and real-time *sensitivity to operations* that allows the people in the process to be aware and learn from the process as it is being performed.

This overemphasis on standard work with underemphasis on capturing the intellect and dynamic discovery and adjustment by expertise local is *not* indicative of an HRO. In fact, overemphasizing standard work is often a result of the opposite behaviors of leaders in HROs.

Standard Work's Role in Reliability

The leaders of HROs know that continuous improvement is key to reliability, both in achieving high reliability and sustaining reliability. Thus, it brings me to a discussion of what I hear almost every day in healthcare organizations whose staff and leaders were trained by consultants who claim to be *Lean consultants*: "The solution is standard work."

The leaders in HROs trust their staff to do what is right for the patient. When insecure about their own staff's ability to achieve the reliability that is needed, leaders are the problem. Leaders allowed a system to evolve where the people doing the work do not have the resources to do it reliably if they do not know what is right for the patient.

Leadership who keep touting the standard work mantra are also the ones who say that they just need to reeducate the staff. These misguided managers are often known to be auto-cratic managers who destroy high reliability.

Let us start with where the term standard work origi-nated. I have included material from the original authors of *Training within Industry* (1945),[3] which developed *stan-dardized work (SW)*. Immediately, we see that even the term *standard work* has been modified from its original term. That is not reliable.

Lean as it is used here is a term that was coined by a group at the Massachusetts Institute of Technology (MIT) who stud-ied the automotive industry. In the book *The Machine That Changed the World,*[4] Daniel Roos, James Womack and Daniel Jones (1991) shared the origins of the term. Lean describes the Toyota processes that were compared to Ford, General Motors (GM), and Chrysler processes. The amount of time and resources to do similar tasks at Toyota were much less than at Ford, GM, and Chrysler. The term *Lean* applied to Toyota was coined by an MIT student who studied under the direction of Womack.

The so-called standard work is touted too often as not standard work at all. It is the method that the boss says is the right way. Is any method standard work if it does not result in the level of reliability that can be achieved? Toyota defines standard work as the method that achieves reliability in the time allowed, with just the right amount of inventory. Standard work that does not achieve the patient's desired outcome is hardly standard work.

> Today's standardization ... is the necessary foun-dation on which tomorrow's improvement will be based. If you think of "standardization" as the best you know today, but which is to be improved tomorrow—you get somewhere. But, if you think of standards as confining, then progress stops.[5]

Standard work's three elements further exemplify its contribution to reliability. In Figure 5.1,[6] the three elements of standard work using healthcare's primary mission as an example are

1. The right tasks to accomplish the clinical outcome and in the correct sequence
2. The tasks performed in the required time
3. Having the resources to accomplish the tasks in the correct sequence at the right time

Let us add some examples of lack of reliability by sharing examples of standard work that are not being achieved:

1. How many times has failure occurred because any one of these three standard work elements was not achieved? Doing the wrong surgical procedure? Compounding a medicine in the incorrect sequence?
2. Not allowing enough time for a handover between two caregivers is an example of not meeting takt time. Takt time is simply the time that is necessary for a task to occur to meet the customer's needs/demands.
3. Running out of supplies in preparing to discharge a patient is an all-too-common example of the third element that is necessary for standard work—resources. Human resources is another sad state of affairs.

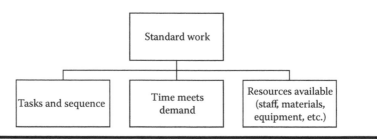

Figure 5.1 Standard work elements. (From Monden, Y., *Toyota Production System*, Second Edition, Institute of Industrial Engineers, 1993, p. 146.)

I have wasted countless hours reeducating leaders who emphasize creating documents under the directive, "We need to create standard work." Yet, there is little-to-no validation that the so-called standard work documents describe methods that result in achieving the expected, or even best, outcomes. At best, perhaps some documents might have helped in one instance in a small hospital with no assurance of cause and effect or even correlation. These same leaders often present an even worse situation. They make everyone else comply with one person's opinion of standard work and ignore the ideas of others who might have a better method and data to support that their methods actually meet all the three requirements of standard work. The eighth waste is the waste of intellect, which destroys continuous improvement—the very essence of what makes HROs more reliable than their competitors.

Standardized Work History

"In Lean Manufacturing, you must fight your current thinking when it comes to the conventional wisdom of work standards. In doing so, you may make the leap to a different understanding of Standardized Work. These mental gymnastics are very difficult to achieve through shop floor practice however; mainstream Standardized Work training is very limited and current business trends tend to follow the mainstream. It is an uphill battle for Lean practitioners to work at implementing true standard work."[7]

Here is what we know about SW based on Toyota literature[5]:

Standardized work is ideally never static.

An actual example is from a time when two consultants from the same organization worked independently in two different health systems, helping leaders understand the need for frequent visual management of key metrics. The by-product of these two contracts was to be the firm's standard work to be shared across healthcare in how to organize and display metrics. I picked this true story because one cannot over-emphasize the importance of leaders measuring, displaying, and managing to the critical measures, such as slips and mistakes in surgical services and abandoned calls in a support center, which schedules procedures. In my first book, *Utilizing the 3Ms of Process Improvement in Healthcare* (2012), I shared examples on the front cover of leaders and staff managing to the measures that are posted in their surgical unit and customer set. Thus, having standard work for leaders to know how to utilize measurement, managing to the measure, and making it easier for staff to continuously improve seems like time that is well spent.

One consultant, let us use the name Al, and his boss claimed victory early and began writing the standard work and training for the firm. There were no data other than saying that the boards were up in some units. I happened to visit the site for other reasons, and Al was proud to show me the boards with metrics. I saw the boards with charts on them with out-of-date metrics and in monthly granularity, which is not frequent enough for managing to these measures such as quality and productivity.

Months later, I spoke with the other consultant, aka Julie, and saw her presentation showing boards with the daily updated metrics laid out in a reasonable flow of conversation that one would appreciate in a huddle between unit leaders and staff. Julie told me that she had toured Al's site and found the same weaknesses that I saw. Julie told me that no one had reached out to see what she and her client accomplished. And, she was distraught that Al and his group started writing the standard work, and she knew that she would be pressured to use his materials and not hers despite her method being the only one that achieved the desired outcomes—measures that were important, kept updated, and displayed so that all knew the status every day, and they could manage to the measures with confidence.

The leaders of HROs know that standard work is only called as such if it is done the right way. For Al and his boss to claim their standard work to be the only way for the rest of the organization to teach clients was not only not best for the clients; it was also frustrating to many others and slowed their ability in helping the clients. And, it resulted in hours of wasted debate for months about who had the right to determine the standard work and what it was to be.

A culture of high reliability is one that includes others and reinforces the better ways. Not only was the documentation of Al's work weak due to poor results and errors in concept; Julie and others also saw the unilateral decision making in the standard work. They were disheartened and felt that their voices were ignored. Al and his boss had never led an HRO, yet Julie had. In fact, she had a very high level position leading quality in one of the better sites of a world-class firm that you would recognize.

Healthcare Leaders in Practice

Brent James, MD, the chief quality officer and executive director of the Institute for Health Care Delivery Research, Intermountain Healthcare, another leader in healthcare and one mentioned in my book, *Utilizing the 3Ms of Process Improvement in Healthcare* (2012), has taught quality to many in healthcare. His method of including others while developing better practices works. Using Al and Julie again, Dr. James's method probably would have him and the decision makers realize that they need to have better methods for visual management. He would recognize not only Al but also

Julie and would provide a culture where both can experiment in creating a system of visual management, leading to creating standard work for others to follow. The decision on the better method to become the standard would be well understood in advance. Data would determine the better method. Shutting one method down and approving the other's methods without data go against Dr. James's methods. He lets outcomes decide the better method. Well-defined criteria would be established for the visual management outcome, such as actual improvement in the metrics, acceptance by both the frontline staff and their managers, and ability to control and sustain the boards.

Visual Management of and for Reliability

The last criteria are critical in visual management. In the HROs where I worked, such as Eaton Electrical, the visual management boards were always updated and current. How we did this evolved. We started out like many in healthcare using manually updated spreadsheet charts and handwritten whiteboards. This standard work became universal across the large site, and eventually, we worked out the bugs in keeping it current. Once simplified, our information technology group controller, Al Houser, worked to automate the measures and posting.

Receiving the key measures every day was virtually effortless for everyone from the leadership to anyone with a sign-on. And, we made it more difficult not to see the visual management board. At first sign-on, all of the measures would be the first thing to pop up on the screen—and anyone who had a sign-on received the measures, not just leadership. In fact, there was no way to bypass the measures showing. One could also bring the measures back, and many of them would be updated throughout the day, such as orders from customers, stock levels, and inventory levels.

Imagine a surgical services schedule being updated in real time and the inventory of sterile supplies for each procedure being validated before the case starts. The good news is that there are systems now that are not only real-time scheduling display systems; they also reschedule the following cases based on defined constraints such as the surgeon. If a surgeon's case is going longer than planned, his or her subsequent cases will be automatically rescheduled, and notices can be sent.

I am all for simplicity, but it seems not so easy to me that so many surgical operations still use a whiteboard that is updated by busy staff where only those in the area can see the schedule. I cannot imagine running a manufacturing plant in the 1980s this way. And, our customers expected our customer support personnel to have real-time status of their orders, which they had by simply looking at their monitors. In some of the operating room systems, they, too, provide real-time status to the patient's loved ones who can see the progress all along the way from admission to recovery. HROs keep the voice of the customer ever in mind.

We did not need technology to achieve visual management, but HROs recognize that making visual management easier allows human resources to be applied more directly to patient care.

The following story is about a visual management problem that we never solved. It is one of the most common issues in inpatient care settings.

White boards, the same board that we see in restaurants, meeting rooms, fitness centers, and countless other public and private places that allow staff to write and erase, are also mounted in patient rooms in the majority of hospital rooms I have worked. Often, the white boards have defined areas for important information for the clinicians and staff to handwrite updates. These fields include: room number, physician's name, nurse's name, "plan for the day," planned discharge date and time, and special needs.

Here is the problem. I can't name one facility in which the white boards were updated. Often, the discharge date is missing, the attending nurse's name has not been updated, and worse, patients have told me they really value having the boards updated. So, why the problem? It is easy to handwrite the information and patients value the boards. In speaking with staff about not updating the boards, they share that, "they just didn't have time," or "no one looks at it," or "they don't see any value in the board."

Utilizing the 3Ms is always missing when we don't see the boards used well. No one is measuring the staff in keeping them updated, nor is leadership managing-to-the-measure to achieve compliance. Here, I think, is the answer—the 3rd M. It may seem easy to update the boards, but this is relative. Virtually every field on nearly every board I have seen has data that is in a computer. Why on earth do we ask highly skilled staff to manually write on a board information that is, for the most part, kept up-to-date in a computer? Why can't we stream this information on the monitor that is also in every patient's room and easily accessible by punching a button on a remote? Or as a screen saver? Once we use technology that has been around a long time, we can also let the patient and staff interact with the system, such as letting the patient update his or her pain measurement. Every white board I have seen has the emoji-style pain scale. Then, this simple breakthrough could interface with the call system to alert the nurse to come visit.

Visual management is key in high reliability. We have to make it easier and quit wasting staff members' time and intellect.

I see this scenario happen too often in healthcare. Some of the reasons leaders are reluctant to behave as HRO leaders do are the following:

- Do not know how to behave to lead HROs because they have never been in one
- Feel that including others will delay progress

- Not aware of others' abilities
- Insecure about their own work
- Do not value the intellect of others
- Dictatorial

Leaders who overemphasize inspecting frontline staff work may profess to know what makes HROs work. No, when those outside the process look at the outcomes of the frontline staff, that is inspection. Auditing is when these *others* outside of the front line observe the process of the frontline workers. Auditing is to *inspect* how the process and its controls are performing. There is a big difference both in purpose and respect for the staff doing the work. What is worse is when management has not given the staff the resources to know quality as they perform such as not having real-time visual management of the outcome of their work. One example in healthcare is the amount of volume required in a sample drawn by a phlebotomist for the laboratory to properly test. I have witnessed a laboratory director teaching the phlebotomists herself. Before, managers were preparing to inspect phlebotomists to make sure that they had the correct volume. Inspection was prevented by simply sharing the needs between two peers. Having respect for the frontline staff is to

- Train them in quality and reliability as I share in this book
- Give them the tools to achieve such
- Rely on them to inspect their own outcomes—and in real time

Auditing serves the purpose of ensuring that all the three requirements of a quality management system for the frontline staff are sufficient. Specifically, this means that training, resourcing, and the ability to assess outcomes are adequate and in place.

Leading Change with Training within Industry[7]

In my books, *Utilizing the 3Ms of Process Improvement* (2012) and *Utilizing the 3Ms of Process Improvement in Healthcare* (2012), I share specific techniques in leading change from some of the world's greatest leaders and what I have seen in my career. In reviewing the original U.S. government documents on *Training within Industry* (1945), I was struck again with the lessons that we forget and the waste when we do not learn from history.

In the following section, I inserted the actual bulletins that add to the reality that what many think a certain automobile manufacturer invented is really a creation of a U.S. wartime effort to increase the capability and reliability of production and services. These principles are most likely built from the even-older and more universal *Golden Rule*.

The WAY *You Make Improvements Is of First Importance*

Go back in your memory as a workman.

Remember the time you "put up" with a job even though it was awkward and caused you needless trouble and worry? Remember the "better way" you finally worked out which would have made it safer and easier to do? Remember how you wanted to tell your boss about your idea but he wasn't the kind of a fellow who was easy to talk to, and you never mentioned it to him?

Or perhaps, you remember the time when the boss "sprung" *his* new method on you and you had a pretty tough time "swallowing" it.

You will *never* forget the time when the boss "had an idea" and asked you for *your* opinion about it, and how you made several good improvements in his plan and how pleased you were.

Then go back over your experience as a supervisor.

Remember the time you put a new idea "up to the boss?" It was rather poorly worked out and he found a "bug" in your plan right off? And you didn't propose any more.

Remember the time you *really* had a good plan, but you neglected to get some of your fellow supervisors and engineers "in on it" and the plan fell flat?

Then, of course, you will *never* forget the "better way" you worked out, that *was* put into effect and that *did* work. You still can feel the satisfaction that it gave you.

How to Improve Job Methods

Better job methods are needed *now*—desperately so—but there is a *right way* to make them. Here is the plan. It has worked in thousands of cases, and in practically every kind of industry. There are FOUR STEPS to follow. No one step can be omitted. No one step is more important than the other.

STEP I. *BREAK DOWN* the job.

1. List *all* the details of the job *exactly* as done by the Present Method.
2. Be sure details include all
   Material Handling
   Machine Work
   Hand Work
   - take any job—take the first one you see in your department.
   - just "start right in"—jot down on a sheet of paper every *detail* as it happens. Do this right at the job. Don't try to do it back at your desk. You'll overlook something if you do.
   - don't be secretive or mysterious about it. Tell your workers what you are doing. Be frank and open about the listing of details.

STEP II. *QUESTION* every detail.

1. Use these types of questions:

   WHY is it necessary?

   WHAT is its purpose?

   WHERE should it be done?

   WHEN should it be done?

   WHO is best qualified to do it?

   HOW is "the best way" to do it?

2. Also question the

   Materials, Machines, Equipment, Tools, Product Design, Layout, Work Place, Safety, Housekeeping.

   - just start down your sheet of details. Start questioning each one.
   - you won't get far, usually, until some improvements will occur to you.
   - perhaps a BETTER WAY will flash into your mind. Hold this "new idea" temporarily and question EVERY DETAIL on your list before you start to "dope out" the better way. If you stop to work your "flash," you may help only *a part* of the job, and overlook a *broader* or *more useful* improvement.

STEP III. *DEVELOP* the new method.

1. ELIMINATE *unnecessary* details.

2. COMBINE details when practical.

3. REARRANGE details for better sequence.

4. SIMPLIFY all *necessary* details.

   a. Make the work *easier* and *safer.*

   b. Pre-position materials, tools, and equipment at the best places in the proper work area.

   c. Use gravity-feed hoppers and drop-delivery chutes when practical.

   d. Let both hands do useful work.

   e. Use jigs and fixtures instead of hands for holding work.

5. WORK OUT your idea WITH others.

6. Write up your proposed new method.
   - eliminating unnecessary details prevents waste of materials and manpower.
   - combining and rearranging overcome "back tracking" and double handling.
   - simplifying makes the job easier and safer to do.
   - be sure to get all those concerned "in on" your idea from the start. Don't work out the new method and "spring it" on your people. This applies to your boss, your associates, and *particularly to your workers.* The best way of all is to *work out* your idea *with* them. Make them *a part* of it.

STEP IV. *APPLY* the new method.
1. *Sell* your proposal to the *boss.*
2. *Sell* the new method to the *operators.*
3. Get final approval of all concerned on Safety, Quality, Quantity, and Cost.
4. Put the new method to work. Use it until a *better* way is developed.
5. Give *credit* where credit is due.
   - the boss must be "sold" to get his approval for a trial run.
   - the operator may need to know more about it to give the new method a fair test.
   - the new method can yield increased production only after it's actually working.
   - remember, today's best way, is only for today. Tomorrow there will be a better way—and *you* will work it out!
   - stealing an idea is really a form of sabotage. Be open-minded to suggestions, even if many of them are "wild ideas." A really good one will come along that can contribute to victory.

Often a new method will "pop" into your mind without working through these FOUR STEPS. This is to be expected at the start. However, these "flashes" will soon be exhausted.

Don't expect them to continue. For consistent improvement, you must think your way carefully through ALL of the FOUR STEPS. You will have to dig beneath the surface for most of your improvements.

Make the Job Easier and Safer

Remember, your purpose is to make jobs easier and safer—NOT to make people work *harder* or *faster.* This is *NOT* a speed-up plan. It IS to show people how to work more effectively. Keep this basic purpose clearly in mind and you can't fail. Furthermore, you will find "improving job methods" is an interesting undertaking. Most important of all is the fact that you will contribute to VICTORY!

References

1. Libuser, C. B. 1994. *Organization Structure and Risk Mitigation.* Dissertation submitted in partial satisfaction of the requirements for the degree of Doctor of Philosophy in Management. Los Angeles: University of California.
2. Spear, S. 2009. *Chasing the Rabbit. How Market Leaders Outdistance the Competition and How Great Companies Can Catch Up and Win.* New York: McGraw-Hill Companies.
3. National Archives, Records of the War Manpower Commission. 1945. *Training within Industry.* 211.22.4 (Record Group 211) 1936–47.
4. Roos, D., Womack, J. and Jones, D. 1991. *The Machine That Changed the World; The Story of Lean Production.* Harper Perennial.
5. Ford, H. 2004. *The Toyota Way; 14 Management Principles from the World's Greatest Manufacturer.* New York: McGraw Hill, p. 141.
6. Monden, Y. 1993. *Toyota Production System*, Second Edition. Institute of Industrial Engineers, p. 146.
7. Training within Industry Institute website. Available at http://trainingwithinindustry.net/SW.html.

Chapter 6

Achieving Higher Reliability in Functional Outcomes

Utilizing measurement, managing to the measure, and making it easier in achieving higher reliability start with knowing truth in measurement.

Reliability Begins with Truth in Measurement

Measurement systems themselves improve reliability in healthcare. In cardiology, St. Jude Medical manufactures a device that is called optical coherence tomography (OCT) technology. OCT is a measurement system that improves the decision making of a cardiologist in choosing if a stent will have the intended outcome. If OCT as a measurement system is not reporting to the cardiologist information that is correct, the cardiologist may make a less-than-ideal decision such as intervening and placing a stent when the vessel does not benefit from a stent. In reliability, the measurement system itself is a critical component as it is in this cardiology procedure.

This case study includes a machine that is used in making medical devices such as magnetic resonance imaging (MRI)s; robotic surgical systems; and in the heating, ventilating, and air-conditioning (HVAC) systems that manage the temperature throughout the hospital including the surgical suites where infections may increase when the ambient temperature is not reliable. These devices are called motor starters, which are electrical switching and safety devices that are critical in the operation of the machines that make the medical devices and operate the HVAC systems in the healthcare site. Motor starters are also used in the machinery that makes the car that you ride in; the airplane that speeds you to other continents; and the spacecraft that Neil Armstrong, Jim Aldrin, and Michael Collins navigated to the moon and back. Their primary purpose is to improve the reliability of the machines by improving the startup of electrically driven production and conveying equipment. Westinghouse had developed an intelligent motor starter named Advantage that sensed dynamically the power that is needed to start the production machinery and then to start the machine with just enough power to start the equipment. This *soft start* intelligence improved the reliability of the production equipment by reducing the wear on the equipment that occurs with every startup.

The defect was an unreliable measurement of the current, which in turn determined the amount of energy that is needed to start the actual production machine. We knew that the device was not calibrating itself reliably, but we did not know why. I was told that the production equipment that made the actual motor starter was very sensitive to magnetic fields that were caused by the wiring of the test and calibration equipment on the Advantage production line. When I arrived at the plant that made the Advantage starter, there were elaborate harnesses holding the wiring in place, so it did not move.

Signs were also on the machine to not touch the wires for fear of affecting the calibration of the motor starter. I worked with some of the brightest engineers, the suppliers of production equipment, and one of the original developers of the ground fault circuit interrupter (GFCI), Dr. Guenter B. Finke.

The GFCI stops the current flow in a circuit or receptacle in your home and workplace to protect people from electrical shock. A similar technology is used by Motorola Semiconductor, which produced the microprocessor chip in the motor starter that converted the current to voltage dynamically to soft start the production equipment. This is a lesson in ensuring that the measurement system is reliable first before using the measurements to validate how reliable the device or service you are providing really is.

I knew that there was variation in what the motor starter was using to determine how soft the start is. The microprocessor was programmed to read current, convert the current to voltage using a simple linear equation that is known to all electrical engineers, and dynamically start the production equipment. It seemed to me that there was something wrong with the output of this equation, so I spoke with the Motorola sales engineer. She was certain that the microprocessor was operating correctly, so I went back to other causes. While still unable to determine the source of the error, I was able to mathematically derive the correct output when I found a bias to add to the linear equation. By this time, however, I had to leave the project to take on other work.

A month or so later, the product engineer called me with exciting news. The team found out that the equation in the microprocessor had an error. The simple equation of a line you may remember is $Y = mx + b$. The bias I had calculated got the correct answer, and now it made sense why. The manufacturer of the microprocessor had made an error hard coding this equation into the device: $Y = m(x + b)$. Hard coding is programming that cannot be changed in the current microprocessor, so we were stuck with this error. The engineer found a permanent work around the error, and the team solved the issue after months of root cause analysis. And, our failure to stay with a hunch and validate the measurement of current and conversion using the equation were correct. The moral of the story is do not short-cut doing a measurement system analysis even if experts tell you that everything is fine.

Now, let us take this lesson and apply it to healthcare's patient experience measurement system, the Hospital Consumer Assessment of Healthcare Providers and Systems (HCAHPS). I was improving the HCAHPS score at a healthcare system on the West Coast. Every one of the eight questions used to compare this hospital with thousands of other hospitals in the United States showed this hospital to be worse than the national median on all eight questions. Being below the national median on all eight scores is not that improbable, yet I learned to never trust a measurement system. Before we started down a deep time-consuming root cause analysis, we knew to ensure that the scores the hospital was receiving back from the Centers for Medicare & Medicaid (CMS) and its third-party survey administration supplier were correct. By the way, being below the national median on all eight scores was costing this hospital $200,000 every year in CMS' value-based purchasing (VBP). CMS' intent is to drive improvement in clinical quality, patient experience, and cost, and there is no doubt that VBP has been effective in driving improvement.

What I found was that on some months, I could reproduce exactly the scores of the third-party supplier who actually conducted the surveys of patients and reported back to the healthcare organization the scores. However, on some months, I could not reproduce the values. We had to reconcile why the measurement system was returning different values before we went on. In summary, reliability improvement teams must ensure the reliability of the measurement systems that are used in gauging the reliability of the product or service.

Improving Patient Experience Using Reliability Techniques

Patient experience is much about knowing expectations. Reliability is measured using expectations of outcomes over time, right? When these expectations are not met, such as expectations that are shattered when a patient has an unplanned readmission days after discharge while on a well-deserved vacation abroad, how can an unreliable organization expect high patient experience scores?

We have been able to raise patient experience scores using the concepts in this book. Reliability analysis is useful for services, as well as products and clinical procedures. Building on the story of readmissions and infections, we routinely look beyond the inpatient or outpatient stay to understand how reliable the patient's and family's experiences are. Can one imagine that an unplanned return to the hospital would not affect the likelihood to recommend the clinicians and the organization?

Answering patient calls for help is an example of using reliability methods. The teams have raised the patient experience scores that are used to compare hospitals from the 40th percentile to the 85th percentile. We also deploy a longer-term look at the patient experience than the time after discharge that CMS requires for surveying patients. We see failures beyond the prescribed period that can help us identify the root causes that might be contributing to other patients who are yet to experience our care. And, the patients may be even more distraught thinking that their recovery is perfect while within the 30 days.

Pay for Quality versus Fee for Service Driving Need for High Reliability

CMS finalized a rule in November 2015 that total knee and total hip replacements will be paid in a bundled payment in nearly 70 geographic regions instead of the decades-old practice of paying based on the services that are provided.[1] Paying based on the services provided is called *fee for service* and allows acute care hospitals where the surgery was performed to charge for all services that are provided, which allows variation in the payment from CMS to the hospital. CMS wants to shift from 100% fee for service to quality-based reimbursement to drive higher reliability and lower healthcare costs. The actual announcement is in Figure 6.1.

Total knee replacement procedures numbered 719,000 in 2010 according to the CDC/National Center for Healthcare Statistics (NCHS) National Hospital Discharge Survey 2010.[2]

Comprehensive Care for Joint Replacement Model

The Comprehensive Care for Joint Replacement (CJR) model aims to support better and more efficient care for beneficiaries undergoing the most common inpatient surgeries for Medicare beneficiaries: hip and knee replacements (also called lower extremity joint replacements or LEJR). This model tests bundled payment and quality measurement for an episode of care associated with hip and knee replacements to encourage hospitals, physicians, and post-acute care providers to work together to improve the quality and coordination of care from the initial hospitalization through recovery.

The proposed rule for the CJR model was published on July 9, 2015, with the comment period ending September 8, 2015. After reviewing nearly 400 comments from the public on the proposed rule, several major changes were made from the proposed rule, including changing the model start date to April 1, 2016. The final rule was placed on display on November 16, 2015 and can be viewed at the Federal Register.

Background

Hip and knee replacements are the most common inpatient surgery for Medicare beneficiaries and can require lengthy recovery and rehabilitation periods. In 2014, there were more than 400,000 procedures, costing more than $7 billion for the hospitalizations alone. Despite the high volume of these surgeries, quality and costs of care for these hip and knee replacement surgeries still vary greatly among providers.

You can read the proposed rule in the Federal Register at https://innovation.cms.gov /initiatives/cjr. We encourage all interested parties to submit comments electronically through the CMS e-Regulation website at http://www.cms.gov/Regulations-and-Guidance /Regulations-and-Policies/eRulemaking/index.html?redirect=/eRulemaking or on paper by following the instructions that are included in the proposed rule. Submissions must be received by November 16, 2015.

For more information, please visit the CCJR Model web page.

Figure 6.1   CMS announcement, November 16, 2015.

What do patients want in a total knee replacement? They want more mobility and often less pain—the outcome. And, they want the outcome to last their lifetime or at least what the expected duration is according to their physician. Reliability is therefore having more mobility for 20 years, according to John Meding, MD, study author and attending orthopedic surgeon, the Center for Hip & Knee Surgery, Mooresville, IN.[3]

What Does Not Work in Reliability

Healthcare *helpers* need to understand that reliability analysis is often more complex than what they have been led to believe. There are a number of consultants who sell an expectation that five-day *Kaizen events* are all that the organization needs to do. They sell healthcare leaders on the idea that they do not need people in their organization to know *all that math* or statistical analysis. Some try to fit everything into a five-day Kaizen event. How on earth can anything and everything so complex as improving healthcare mortality, readmissions, safety, and functional outcomes with varying levels of experience in reliability be solved every time in five days? I understand that scoping down is useful, but continuous successive small approximations toward a goal often work much better with less energy and commotion in arranging busy people's calendars. In fact, we prefer the original Quality Circle team approach of small blocks of time and training while working on the problem instead of the "event" that disrupts the workweek. And, the team can better learn a process if it can study the process and interact with it during times when it better represents the patients' experiences. Five day kaizen events often misrepresent the actual capability of the process due to a condensed data collection time allowance. We often use meetings only to share with leadership and colleagues while spending most of the team's time in the processes with our patients and staff.

And, some in healthcare can get lulled into sleep by just meeting the standards, such as just meeting the 30-day readmission minimum ratios and claiming reliability. The standards in healthcare are often the minimum acceptable practices. High-reliability organizations take a different mindset and achieve higher reliability as in the example below.

Example

Let's use readmissions of patients who undergo a total knee replacement. CMS was reinforcing looking at the time between discharge and 30 days post-discharge. Anywhere from 2% to over 15% of these patients may need to return to an acute care hospital due to infections, injury, and other issues. When one looks at the count of patients, or rate of patients, readmitted, we see another increase in readmissions between 30 and 90 days. These later readmissions can highlight different root causes than the causes that required readmission prior to 30 days. Thus, different solutions are often needed to improve the outcomes. Meeting the standard of zero admissions between discharge and 30 days is only meeting the standard. It is not providing capable and reliable healthcare.

References

1. Health and Human Services News. 2015. Comprehensive Care for Joint Replacement Model. Available at https://innovation.cms.gov/initiatives/cjr.
2. CDC. 2015. National Hospital Discharge Survey: 2010 table, Procedures by selected patient characteristics—Number by procedure category and age [PDF—38 KB]. Available at http://www.cdc.gov/nchs/fastats/inpatient-surgery.htm.
3. American Academy of Orthopaedic Surgeons. 2011. Total knee replacement patients functioning well after 20 years, study finds. Available at http://www.sciencedaily.com/releases/2011/02/110217082925.htm.

Chapter 7

Achieving Higher Reliability in Safety Outcomes

Safety Engineering

Safety engineering uses a term to help assess the robustness of the system. Factor of safety (FoS), or safety factor (SF), describes the capability of the system to operate beyond its intended operating environment. The SF is how much extra force can be applied to the system before failure occurs. To achieve high reliability with significant variation, we design in an SF. How much SF is needed is dependent on the risks that we will accept.

We hope that healthcare processes are designed with some FoS, at least the ones that could result in harm or death if variation occurs. The failure of the electrical generating system at Langone is an example where the SF was not sufficient because electricity failed to flow despite a backup system. As a result of the system failure, patients had to be relocated to other sites.[1]

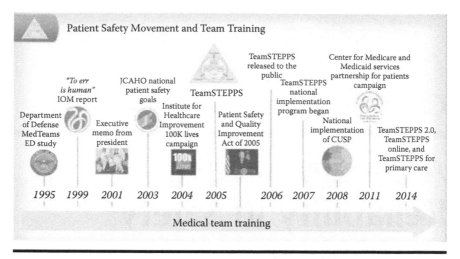

Figure 7.1 Timeline of the patient safety movement and team training. CUSP, Comprehensive Unit-based Safety Program; ED, Emergency Department; IOM, Institute of Medicine; JCAHO, The Joint Commission. (From http://www.ahrq.gov/professionals /education/curriculum-tools/cusptoolkit/modules/learn/index.html.)[3]

TeamSTEPPS

Team strategies and tools to enhance performance and patient safety (TeamSTEPPS)[2] was created to improve healthcare's reliability in safety. The Agency for Healthcare Research and Quality and Department of Defense originally released TeamSTEPPS in 2006, and I found the training to be very professionally done with many techniques that any healthcare organization could implement quickly. Video vignettes put the learner in real-life healthcare situations—and very common ones for hospitals. See Figure 7.1 for a timeline of the patient safety movement.

A Texas-Based Healthcare System on the Path to Higher Reliability across Its System[3]

The team at CHRISTUS utilized the 3Ms of process improvement in compliance to managing urinary catheters that are

inserted into surgical patients (SCIP-9) every day throughout the project and continue to measure daily. The 3Ms are
measure, manage to the measure, and make it easier to do
the right thing. The leaders in higher-reliability healthcare
organizations manage to this measure and support making it
easier to comply. Evidence shows that infections are reduced
if urinary catheters are removed within two days of surgery
and carefully managed. In Figure 7.2, the program I developed
to help healthcare organizations improve reliability graphically illustrates performance in key measures of outcomes and
safety. The Centers for Medicare & Medicaid Services (CMS)
gives points that affect reimbursement in its value-based
purchasing pay-for-performance program. Points are awarded
for being above threshold (white) and maximum points for at
or above benchmark (black) as well as for improving in performance (achieved) from baseline (baseline). One sees that
CHRISTUS was below the threshold but improving from baseline. Our goal was to achieve 100% compliance, and higher
reliability, in managing catheters and ultimately in reducing
infections.

High-reliability projects use mapping to understand the
process and especially the inputs and outputs of the steps in
the process. See Table 7.1. The inputs are key to performance
improvement because it is those inputs that must be made reliable to achieve highly reliable outcomes. The actual process
map is shown in Table 7.1. Reliability is about building capability in the process inputs. So, a special map called a SIPOC is

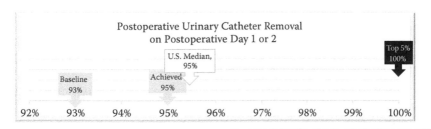

**Figure 7.2   Before work began. Value-based purchasing measures of
CHRISTUS and CMS threshold and benchmark.**

useful. SIPOC is an acronym for a map that lists the suppliers to the process, inputs, process (steps), outputs, and customers. The SIPOC mapping effort often results in quick wins when the team members realize inputs that are going wrong or missing entirely. In SCIP-9, the team realized that the nurses

Table 7.1 Process Map of Catheter Management

Inputs	Process	Output
• Doctors • Nurses • Patient education • Handoff	Preoperative (Review history and physical [H&P])	• Identify patients who will have a foley. • Failure to identify patients who will have a foley.
• Surgeon • Nurse • Handoff	Surgery	• Staff aware of Surgical Care Improvement Project (SCIP)-9 patient. • Staff unaware of SCIP-9 patient.
• Surgeon • Nurse • Handoff	PACU	• Staff aware of SCIP-9 patient. • Staff unaware of SCIP-9 patient.
• Intensivist • Hospitalist • Nurse • Patient or family involvement • Whiteboard communication • Handoff charting	Unit	• Staff aware of SCIP-9 patient. • Staff unaware of SCIP-9 patient.
• Electronic health record documentation • Communication of results • Core measure nurse involvement	Documented compliance	• Catheter removals are compliant. • Catheter removals are not compliant.

caring for patients with urinary catheters often did not know the need to remove the catheter by postoperative day 1. Not every patient falls under the SCIP-9 rule such as patients who undergo urological procedures where the catheter must be maintained beyond postoperative day 2 for healing purposes.

The team drilled down the higher-level reasons for failing to remove the urinary catheter in its analyze phase resulting in the findings of the root cause analysis in Figure 7.3.

The team felt that the root causes circled were the most common ones and developed improvements to the process for these first. They went on to make even more improvements.

Tantamount in this project was building a safety culture. The chief nursing officer, Angie Lambert, and her peers at the other two hospitals working on the project demonstrated high-reliability leadership by stating early in the project and often that she valued people who speak up, regardless of the message. Angie was tested multiple times throughout the year that I was working with them, and each time, she showed support

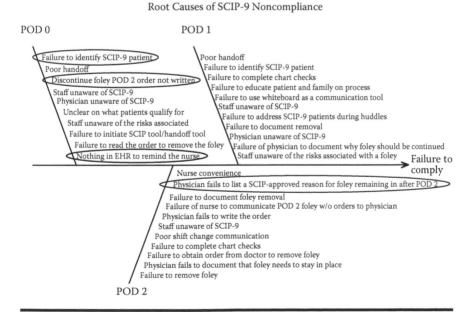

Figure 7.3 **Fishbone chart of potential root causes to noncompliance of catheters. POD, postoperative day.**

for the person reporting close calls. One day, a team member feared that the reason a physician wrote to not remove the catheter was that it was not compliant with CMS rules. Angie could have immediately dismissed the person's concern saying that any reason is good enough. (Actually, CMS requires only a reason and does not qualify its validity.) However, despite the pressure of ruining the streak of days since the project began, she publicly thanked the person for her concern and asked the team to investigate openly and honestly. Even though the *letter of the law* only requires a reason, Angie wanted the true intent of the law to help judge the compliance. Say, for example, a physician ordered the catheter to not be removed at the patient's request. (Some patients prefer a urinary catheter over having to get up and go to the toilet.) This is a risk to the patient and not in his or her overall interest in situations where it is just more convenient for him or her.

After one week of the project (day 5), the hospital region was only 95% compliant in the rule. The national median per CMS was 95%. The three hospitals in this project started achieving 100 compliance almost immediately after identifying and correcting causes see Figure 7.4.

Managing to the measure is a daily task and is critical in healthcare processes that are not fail-safed. In Figure 7.5, Karen, the postoperative recovery nurse, is shown behind the daily chart. The pros of using compliance as a measure are its simplicity and maybe, most importantly, the mindfulness and

Postoperative Urinary Catheter Removal
on Postoperative Day 1 or 2

Top 5%
100%

| | U.S. Median, 95% | | | | Achieved 99% |
Baseline 93%

92%   93%   94%   95%   96%   97%   98%   99%   100%

Figure 7.4   After one week of team reliability improvement work.

Figure 7.5 Frontline staff posting the measure daily and visual management.

awareness that such a measure brings to prevent recurrences of the event.

Also on display is the root cause analysis chart to remind staff how the process could fail and to continuously improve reliability by inviting new root causes to be written.

Achieving 100% Reliability: Case Study

The team had sustained 100% perfect reliability for well over a year. After about 400 days, they had a fallout: noncompliance. Although many were heartbroken, the staff focused on the patients when discovered resulting in no infection. In the true fashion of high-reliability organizations, Angie led the team to identify the root causes. Two contributing factors occurred and had been identified on the failure mode and effects analysis, yet the controls were insufficient, as the team discovered with the fallout. The factors of confusing documentation and confusion in who was monitoring contributed to this fallout. The team leaders of high-reliability organizations react differently to a failure from leaders who continue to struggle to achieve reliability. Angie convened the staff the next day when the fallout was discovered, and the team implemented a stronger, clearer accountability.

References

1. Agency for Healthcare Research and Quality TeamSTEPPS training 2.0.
2. Sifferlin, A. 2012. Time Healthland. Lessons from Storm Sandy: When hospital generators fail in the wake of superstorm Sandy, much of New York City was plunged into darkness. What happened to the patient? Available at http://healthland.time.com/2012/10/30/lessons -from-storm-sandy-when-hospital-generators-fail/.
3. Learn about CUSP. October 2015. Agency for Healthcare Research and Quality, Rockville, MD. http://www.ahrq.gov/professionals /education/curriculum-tools/cusptoolkit/modules/learn/index .html.
4. CHRISTUS Santa Rosa. 2015. *National Patient Safety Foundation 17th Annual National Patient Safety Congress.* April 29–May 1, 2015, Austin, TX.

Chapter 8

The Roadmap
to Higher Reliability

Methodologies Overview

The simplest roadmap in achieving reliability is to:

1. Identify the hazards using failure mode and effects analysis
2. Determine the root causes of the failures
3. Mitigate the failures
4. Continuously reassess and improve

High-reliability organizations (HROs) believe in keeping everything as simple and easy to understand as possible. Deming taught problem solving using the acronym PDCA or plan–do–check–act and based this on Dr. Shewhart's plan–do–study–act. Fortunately, Shewhart and Deming knew to thoroughly define the issue and calculate baseline performance before the PDCA work. Unfortunately, many who followed them misinterpreted that one could go directly to PDCA without clearly defining the issue and having baseline performance to compare the performance during the PDCA to know the effects of the PDCA experiment. The Institute for Healthcare Improvement promotes PDCA with preliminary steps to define the issue and find the baseline performance before PDCA.

PDCA is an acronym that makes it easier to remember the steps in problem solving. Six Sigma's Define, Measure, Analyze, Improve, Control is also known as DMAIC and includes PDCA. DMAIC is easy to remember, and there are other methodologies that are purposely renamed yet following the same steps as DMAIC. Chalk it up to egos, maybe, that companies have to rename the scientific problem-solving steps, but it would be harmless if they follow the steps in order and include an acronym that makes it simpler to remember. What I do not understand are terms for scientific problem solving that do not hint at the steps or use terms that were created for other purposes. *A3 problem solving* is one such term. A3 is the size of a piece of paper and thus the name for a storyboard that Toyota promotes to share an effort with very few pages. Toyota promotes telling the story on one side of an A3 piece of paper. Sometime afterwards, someone started using the term *A3* to denote a problem-solving methodology. Toyota uses the same PDCA cycle and steps that are found in DMAIC going back to its quality circle problem solving that is borrowed heavily from Deming and Ishikawa. Why one thinks naming the scientific problem solving A3 and then having to constantly define the steps seems wasteful to me. Toyota also continues to use the term, "Quality Circles" that is a self-evident term where circles (teams) of frontline staff learn the steps and apply to problems in their work area.

Robust Process Improvement—A Healthcare Problem-Solving Methodology Based on DMAIC

Mark Chassin, president of The Joint Commission (TJC), hired me to compose and deploy what he calls robust process improvement (RPI). My teams and the teams at some of the most reliable healthcare organizations in the United States succeeded in achieving higher reliability in hand hygiene to reduce healthcare-acquired infections, handoff communications for patient safety, and lessen the occurrences of surgical errors, specifically wrong patient, site, and procedures.

"We believe that three sets of process improvement tools— lean, six sigma, and change management—constitute the most effective way for health care to dramatically enhance its capacity to create nearly perfect safety processes.[2] They are proving to be far more effective in addressing complex clinical quality and safety problems than PDCA ('plan, do, check, act') or their more immediate predecessors" (p. 470).[2] "The Joint Commission has adopted RPI as its internal process improvement methodology and, in the first five years of the program, which began in 2008, trained 35% of its workforce in using these tools" (pp. 459–490).[2]

"Since 2009, the Joint Commission Center for Transforming Healthcare has been applying these RPI tools together with teams from hospitals around the country that also have mastered their use to address a number of healthcare's most persistent quality and safety problems. We have found them to be highly effective."[2]

After developing a methodology that is capable of problem solving, one needs to learn it, apply it, and ensure the desired outcomes and scalability. A methodology that only works in a limited number of situations or types of healthcare organizations would never get healthcare as an industry to high reliability. I was confident that RPI would work well because I developed it from proven success in HROs such as United Airlines and Motorola. However, I left before TJC was able to include all of my reliability engineering.

I am very proud of my staff and the many leaders whom we worked with at Johns Hopkins, Mayo Clinic, New York Presbyterian, North Shore Long Island Jewish, Cedars-Sinai, and others who used our roadmap that I originally created when I led the development of United Airlines' Lean Six

Sigma. Frank Masek, my colleague, helped me bring the road-map to life and contributed to the backside that contains many tips and templates for many of the steps on the roadmap.

A High-Reliability Methodology That Works

These are the steps to higher reliability including designing a process and improving it:

1. Defining the purpose of the work to be done
2. Measuring the current state performance
3. Analyzing for root causes to the problem
4. Furthering and piloting improvements to get the desired outcome
5. Controlling the process by ensuring auditing and con-tinual measurement, creating job instructions, tools, and, yes, standard work for leadership to audit the process

   In this book, I covered all of the major methods that are necessary to achieve high reliability. I invented none of them. What I hope to accomplish for you, considering that you are reading this book to achieve high reliability and have found it too daunting so far, is to make it easier. After all, I would not be following my own advice if I did not utilize the third M—make it easier. The roadmap shared in my first book, *Utilizing the 3Ms of Process Improvement in Healthcare* (2012), was designed to achieve high reliability, and the foundation of the roadmap is scientific methodology with Change Leadership. You can download it for free at http://www.rpmexec.com.

   High reliability is dependent on the roadmap being used in companies that supply your healthcare organization, as well as the companies that add value after the patients leave your organization. At the Center for Transforming Healthcare, we did not have the resources or time to teach RPI to all of the upstream and downstream suppliers and customers and stakeholders who served some of the country's highest-quality hospitals. We felt good to have collaborated with 24 hospitals and ambulatory surgical centers in the first three years considering that pilot sites are just a few of the over 5000 acute care hospitals and countless more surgical centers.

However, I could not teach them everything in achieving reliability in the three years that it has taken me now 34 years to learn, try, fail, and refine.

Upstream stakeholders provide services or products that the healthcare organizations use. Downstream stakeholders can be payers, durable medical equipment suppliers, and the next level of care providers. In a total knee arthroscopy, the examples of upstream providers are the laboratory, which measures vital blood parameters, the scheduling office, preadmission instructions staff, and anesthesiology. The surgeon and the perioperative staff with the skills of the anesthesiologist, rely on these upstream stakeholders and processes to have a reliable and safe outcome.

Downstream stakeholders include the recovery staff, therapists, nutritionists, and durable medical equipment manufacturers. This is by no means a complete list; in fact, it is a very small portion of all of the parties who are involved in achieving high reliability. Thus, we see that one definition of complexity is the number of organizations that are involved with healthcare.

Achieving high reliability in any one organization is a function of the reliability of those organizations upstream and downstream. This is why Chassin and others have found it difficult to find any healthcare organization that has achieved high reliability. Until we have built robustness into any one organization for the variation in products and services before and after the organization, we must also improve the reliability in the entire stream.

In the electrical safety products, and aerospace and automotive industries, high reliability has been achieved throughout the stream for years. For example, as a supplier of circuit breakers that might be the brand that you have in your home, my staff measured the reliability of the suppliers of silver-impregnated contacts, which closed and opened to allow or stop the flow of electricity when an unsafe condition was occurring. If the silver contacts failed the electrical circuit may generate excessive heat due to poor electrical contact. This heat may open the circuit via the breaker's mechanism which is a fail-safe condition and stop the flow of current. Worse, the contacts could weld closed keeping the flow of current continuing, negating the breaker's mechanism, resulting in high heat and possible fire.

The next step is to start teaching the methodology.

References

1. Available at http://www.rpmexec.com/#!undefined/sitepage_2.
2. Chassin, M. R. and Loeb, J. M. 2013. High reliability health care: Getting there from here. *The Milbank Quarterly* 91(3): 459–490, http://doi.org/10.1111/1468.0009.12023.

Chapter 9

Quality Leaders and Reliability

W. Edwards Deming

In *The Essential Deming: Leadership Principles from the Father of Quality* (2013),[1] W. Edwards Deming shares his secret for the United States when overseas competition was greatly affecting the U.S. industry. He wrote that if you believe that healthcare is in a crisis, the secret is "Management of a system, cooperation between components, not competition. Management of people" (p. 17).

Market share was being lost by U.S. companies when Deming wrote his book *Out of Crisis* (1982) to those who were competing on quality and continuously improving processes that improved margins. Whether or not you believe that U.S. healthcare is in a crisis, Figure 1.3 suggests that similar competitive pressures happen in healthcare today that existed when Deming and others believed that U.S. industries were in a crisis to survive.

Profound Knowledge

Hard work and best efforts, put forth without guidance of profound knowledge, lead to ruin the world that we are in today. There is no substitute for knowledge. What is profound knowledge? An attempt to supply some answers follows.

The System of Profound Knowledge[1] appears here in four parts, all related to each other:

1. *Appreciation for a system.* Deming helped leaders move away from optimizing the components of a process or organization without taking into account how these many components interact.
2. *Theory of variation states that everything will vary, and understanding this and making processes more robust to the variation are key to reliability.*
3. *Theory of knowledge is the element containing Deming's plan–do–check–act continuous learning and improvement cycle, which was originally created by Shewhart.*
4. *Psychology or understanding what motivates people to want to do a good job.* Deming believed that this fourth element is the most important and most difficult.

Deming goes on to write about evil styles of management, which helps us in Chapters 4 and 7 detail the safety culture that is also necessary to achieve high reliability. Those evils include ranking people, creating competition among staff, and failure to understand cooperation in a system in which everybody wins.

Understanding high reliability in the context of a system, process, and safe operation leads us to understanding robustness. Robustness is what all high-reliability organizations (HROs) have achieved. Robustness makes systems reliable. Being robust means achieving the desired outcome throughout the expected time *despite* variation occurring. How does a system achieve robustness? It begins again with a systems approach.

Reliability and Six Sigma—An Interview with Mikel Harry, Cofounder of Six Sigma

Our quality stinks.

Art Sundry
Motorola

The story of Six Sigma is a story of high reliability. Mikel Harry agreed to share with us in an interview from 2015 why he and Motorola developed Six Sigma. My purpose in speaking with Dr. Harry is to share lessons from Motorola in its quest for reliability that many of you see the result in first responder radios. And, his tale is the tale of all the HROs where I have worked and led, which includes a high-reliability turnaround as lessons for leaders and staff in healthcare who are striving to become a more reliable organization.[2]

Rick: Mikel, please share Motorola's situation prior to you and Bill* developing Six Sigma.

Mikel: Rick, I know that your book is about how to improve reliability in healthcare. Let me start with the fact that we (Motorola) were a high-reliability company. We were known for reliability in our police and fire radios. Motorola owned the market globally in mission-critical products including first responder radios, which are found in many healthcare facilities and police and fire departments globally. It (high-reliability) might have been true in the beginning, but we expanded sales without expanding quality at the same proportion or better. We were losing to the Japanese. We owned the market for car radios, hence the name Motor (Motorcar) Ola (Victrola). But, we lost the market in car radios. We had a huge market share

---

* Bill Smith, engineer and the cofounder of Six Sigma, 1929–1993.

in television. We lost the market in television, too. We got a little too big for our boots. Customers started complaining. In 1979, America was losing to Japanese quality. Bob Galvin, the chief executive officer (CEO) of Motorola, asked what was wrong with the country. "Our quality stinks," was voiced by Art Sundry, a Motorola officer. Just about everybody fell over.

To convince more of our leadership, it took a lot of benchmarking data to prove it. The officers accepted it. In the fact-finding process, Bob Galvin went out to speak with the customers. He consistently got the same message: *your quality stinks.*

Rick: We share the definition of reliability in this book and, in my previous books, the definition of quality. How did you describe these terms initially at Motorola and then at GE, Honeywell, Panasonic, and the many organizations that you have helped?

Mikel: Reliability is the capability to sustain quality over time. "Capability is everything." Critical-to-quality characteristics are things that fail. As the total opportunities increase, given a constant capability, failures occur faster.

Rick: Mikel, you just described reliability as quality over time. And, you brought up W. Edwards Deming's concepts of "rolled throughput yield" and his "Theory of Escaping Defects," which are taught in your Six Sigma courses.

Mikel: Yes. We proved him correct at Motorola in our turnaround with Six Sigma. We found a direct correlation between defects that are produced in the product and the total defect count that you make. That was an important finding. It meant that from our test view, we needed to rock, shake, rattle, and roll and try to bring out those defects to pop forward the latent defects. A metaphor is that you look like a teenager with acne—acne being the latent defects.

Rick: Is it primarily just defect opportunities and the number of defects that we need to focus on?

Mikel: In layman's terms, think of complexity, capability, width and control of variation, and a process that is centered. I think in terms of three Cs: (1) control, (2) capability, and (3) complexity. The first two add up to consistency. Quality is equal to consistency. We consistently do the right thing from a service point of view.

The root of failures is the defects that are produced during the process. And, reliability design requires testing. One test is overstress where we take a product beyond its design limits. We found that we very seldom had problems due to overstress.

Rick: Mikel, you are sharing overstress as one type of accelerated test that is used by high-reliability organizations. We used this for electrical safety products, how well our call centers could react during high demand, and before we open a new unit to ensure that we were reliable in our service and to check our understanding of ways to fail so that we could "beef up" our process before startup. An example in health-care of a stress test is what we call a stress test for how our hearts work under physical stress. Just like at Motorola, a stress test may also make it easier to diagnose heart problems when our hearts are working hard and beating fast. Please share more about reliability testing and stress.

Mikel: Yes, overstress is when a product or service is taken beyond its design limits. The marginal overstress passed the design limits in our products. We did not learn enough from simply stress testing to achieve reliability to compete against higher-reliable competitors. What we found was the impact of the third C, complexity. Due to complexity increasing and the opportunities to fail increasing, and because the products and services got close to the design limits, latent defects were getting activated out in the field. The defects we did not pick up in our plants under stress testing, unfortunately, are those that customers would find in use.

Solder joints are a critical-to-quality characteristic, as one can imagine, in military radios, consumer and commercial pagers, and mobile phones. I just described, by the way, two grades of product: commercial grade versus military. Solder joints in military applications are inspected using 50X (50 times magnification) power in military versus an eye loupe. (Think of the device a jeweler uses to inspect your diamond, which is often 10X.) An eye loupe is often the tool that is used to check the quality of a joint in commercial products. The problem with small latent defects is that you don't see some defects without the 50X. When mechanical or electrical energy hits a weak solder joint or component, it will pop at the slightest crack. If your team does not pick up on the small cracks, time, complexity, and stress may. The more poor joints made, and the more you make, the longer it needs to be in test to expose the latent defects. At Motorola, we found that we needed more exposure to draw out the latent defect rates to achieve the high levels of reliability to compete in the world marketplace.

One win came from increasing our understanding of the latent defects from the higher magnification. We exposed the latent defects better and earlier, and we could reduce the time under test that is needed to expose those defects. Testing with an eye loupe would have required extremely long and costly testing. Proper testing and in-process inspection reduce the infant mortality. It all traces back to the manufacturing process, which is not capable.

Rick: Infant mortality. I cringed when I have used that term after leaving Motorola and United Airlines and joined healthcare. Please explain for our readers.

Mikel: Yes, infant mortality is a term that is used in reliability engineering describing a pattern of failures that are found very early in the life of a product or service.

Rick: Infant mortality issues were the first project that Motorola asked me to work on. OnStar, a Motorola invention and installed in millions of GM vehicles, and the similar BMW Assist used in its vehicles were experiencing failures at GM's and BMW's assembly plants—failures that occurred before the vehicle even left the factory—infant mortality. We used Six Sigma and solved the issues and covered this story in my first books, also finding that we need to measure in real time, manage to the measure as the process works, not after failure, and make it easier and easier to achieve quality the first time. Why do we find health-care organizations also reinventing the wheel when it comes to using Six Sigma and similar reliability meth-ods that are used in one of its units and not in others?

Mikel: A sad commentary Rick, and one that I see in health-care occurring today.

Rick: Recently, I was asked about the design for Six Sigma as if it was separate from Define, Measure, Analyze, Improve, Control (DMAIC). Perhaps, share more about the beginning of Six Sigma for our readers.

Mikel: I think that this will clear this up. Bill coined the term Six Sigma. It was about design reliability. Six Sigma was created to see the robustness of design. So, we redesign until we get it robust. That is the design for Six Sigma. Six Sigma was "born in design." It was not born in production.

But, let me start from the beginning to put this in context and address why healthcare workers and others might be confused and frustrated about what Six Sigma is and what it has achieved.

I joined Motorola around 1981. I was an intern working on my doctorate. In 1984, Bill Smith and I met. Bill wrote a little white paper on latent defects and process capability. But, how far is a paper going to go with math in it? Prior to 1984, Motorola launched 10X, which was an improvement program, and then the 100X program, but they flopped.

Rick: Sounds like the Taguchi loss function venerated again where Taguchi suggests that costs increase whenever deviation away from the nominal occurs—not just when a service fails the tolerance.

Mikel: Yes. By applying Six Sigma, we improved capability all along the process, reducing the defects so much that Motorola wiped out all the service centers and told the customers to throw the pager away versus returning it. That was a big "aha." That is how to do it.

Going back, this is what was happening in the design and floor teams. We had been doing statistical process control (SPC) and all that. We needed to go back into design to reduce those defects. We were designing with concurrent engineering with the process design, yet you don't know the process capabilities. Have to postulate the process capabilities.

Rick: We all know that process capability is key. Please connect the design and the process benefits from Six Sigma.

Mikel: Absolutely. The process—we did not know the capabilities, so we fudge-factored something that is known as the 1.5 sigma shift. We had to have a design robust-to-process variation, which is always present. As Deming and others proved, inspection is only 85% effective in detecting defects. We have to factor in test and inspection efficiency. There are costs that are associated with going all the way back to fixing that defect in the field.

The 1.5 sigma shift was what Motorola postulated to address the process variation. To ignore that processes vary and their centers shift is to disregard reality and sacrifice reliability. The 1.5 sigma shift is not a real thing. We derived it empirically, and it has proved to fit well. When we design with it in mind, we get the Six Sigma quality.

The cost of failure, we were shocked to discover, was roughly 15%–20% of sales. So, for an average organization, we were leaving 15%–20% of our sales. Imagine that for a $10-billion company, we were leaving $2 billion on the table. No wonder we were struggling to compete. We thought that they (the Japanese) were product dumping. They were not. They were just building a better mousetrap. Motorola decided to fight. The Bandit was the pager code name where we first applied Six Sigma.

We had faith in Six Sigma's ability to design in reliability and develop processes with high quality. The Bandit design went like this. We took 20–25 design cycles to understand the reliability and capability. We literally changed the production process to not have a test or inspection built in. We put a dumpster at the end of the line. The folks dumped whatever defects occurred into the dumpster. The goal was to get those defects down to a lower level in the dumpster. Talk about a visual management of quality in real time! The team kept improving and eventually lowered the defects ending up in the dumpster.

The pager reliability improved to achieve a mean time to failure (MTTF) of 157 years, and we beat the Japanese. The cost was also lower with an MTTF that is so high. Six Sigma then went on to help us regain our high reliability, which continues today in first responder devices.

Rick: Yes, I see Motorola radios in nearly every hospital that I have worked for, from the West Coast of America to throughout the United Kingdom. I asked if anyone ever had a radio go bad. Zero. Mikel, you have always given credit to Bill for his contribution. At Eaton Corporation, I first heard about you and Bill because of Motorola winning the coveted Malcolm Baldrige Award. It was here that the word really got out about Six Sigma, thanks to Baldrige promoting winners sharing their methods. Unfortunately for me, you had left Motorola before I joined. We all know you went on to help GE and many others benefit from Six Sigma, including Eaton Corporation where I was taught. Can you share more?

Mikel: Yes, Bill had coined the term Six Sigma. Again, it was simply how good we had to be to achieve the reliability to compete against the Japanese who had beat us on quality. The Bandit pager was a success, and we applied Six Sigma. Soon after, we won the Malcolm Baldrige Award and were named the best managed company in the United States. We were a corporate success story. We went from the agony of defeat to the thrill of victory. I owe a lot to Bob Galvin (son of the founder of Motorola) who became my mentor in the company and allowed me to help spread the word.

    Unfortunately, in the midst of our early success in 1993, Bill passed away in the cafeteria. I got charged with leading Six Sigma. At the time of Bill's death, we had a goal of 3.4 defects-per-million opportunities and the name Six Sigma.

    Early on, I put the design optimization methods into print. Motorola University took it and developed the Six Sigma courses, and we began teaching Six Sigma and speaking with companies across the globe.

    When we talked with companies, I was ashamed for them and appalled at companies that had a great reputation yet not reliable. Motorola found how much better we were.

As you said, the Malcolm Baldrige Award promotes winners in sharing. So, I wrote the book, and it sold 500,000 copies.

I had the pleasure of learning from Bill. Soon, we began to help others, especially after winning Baldrige in 1988. Percy Barnevik, the CEO of Asea Brown Boveri (ABB), was so interested in Six Sigma and what we accomplished; he hired me with the support of Bob Galvin. ABB was like 1200 corporations being very decentralized and of average quality. We started and got 6% cost out in the first year. It wasn't long for me to see the potential.

Why am I doing this for others? I decided to commercialize Six Sigma on my own. Larry Bossidy, the CEO of Allied Signal, knew Allied Signal was hurting and used Six Sigma to cure its woes. Jack Welch grabbed Six Sigma and wanted an early win and chose coincidentally GE's medical business. GE Healthcare applied Six Sigma, quickly achieving higher reliability in GE's computed tomography (CT) scanners and x-ray tubes.

Rick: Mikel, thank you for sharing the evolution of Six Sigma and how it changed Motorola and other leading companies. Please share your future plans.

Mikel: The first generation of Six Sigma with Motorola was about defect reduction. This was the primary focus of Six Sigma. In the 1990s, it helped us with cost reduction. Now, in the third generation, it is about the creation of value. So many companies are hung up in the first generation of Six Sigma. They use Six Sigma as a tool instead of the business management system that Six Sigma originally was. Jack believed in Six Sigma because of the following: Six Sigma got reliability the first time. This allowed me (Mikel) to help

GE to reach the control function. I deployed at Sony, Toshiba, and others who may or may not use the term Six Sigma, but it is evident. One could say that their pride was to not have an American term in their company.

One issue is that Six Sigma has really grown as it went out in breadth. But, it is getting lost in depth. The depth is eroding. It is becoming like a floating little island. The root system is eroding. One example is the development of the Black Belt (BB). Originally, I developed this for a Unisys plant manager, Cliff Ames, who saw the value in teaching Six Sigma to his team to accelerate Six Sigma throughout his organization. Later, Jack Welch asked to speed it even further, and that is when we developed the Master Black Belt (MBB) who would go on to teach BBs and others. Today, I see training suggesting that a BB can be trained in five days. This is dilution pollution. The core of what made Six Sigma great was technical and leadership knowledge. Everybody jumped onboard. They had to switch it around, polluting it. Can't even tell the resemblance of Six Sigma in some training and applications. Does not even qualify. The big names in annual 2014 CEO surveys—about 78% of CEOs—are turning their eye toward growth and only 20% on cost reduction. Mergers and acquisition (M and A) or organic is the only way to grow. The M and A did not work. You have to improve the value proposition: quality multiplied by quantity-divided price. The numerator is the bang, and the denominator is the buck. The bang for buck is getting the right quality and quantity at the lowest possible price. No one can beat us then.

Now, we are into an era that Six Sigma has stepped up to the business level. Business. Operation Process Individual. We actually work with Executive MBBs.

They have a business acumen; MBBs often don't.
Seeing a huge demand, allocation of seats is sold.
Basically, we take the business world and merge it
with the technical world, and in that way, the C-Suite
has the vision of Six Sigma. They can practice the Six
Sigma way of thinking. That is where it has been and
where it is going.

Pioneering is the ability to compute process capability from financial data. Now, working financially and
working backwards. Many don't have process data.
But, everyone has financial data. Find hot spots from
the financials. The key is knowing the equations. The
quality of the process cycle, not the product quality.
A machine has a dial. That is a product cycle. Lots of
things can go wrong, but with Y as a function of x, the
defect is a function of the x. Defects are symptomatic
of the process. The figure of merit is the mean time
to intervention of the process. Other things can cause
defects and capacity issues that have nothing to do
with quality. Value is how much quality we get per dollar that we spend. $Y = f(x)$. The heart of Six Sigma. It
resonated with people. The variable f is the transformation. Never was in the quality literature until Six Sigma.

That is kind of the history of Six Sigma, where it is
today, and more toward the need for signal process-
ing rather than SPC. Shewhart's SPC is still very much
needed in healthcare. Yet, why are we still putting
run charts up when we have computers to calculate
the more informative parameters in an SPC chart? It is
insane. It is like using a musket from the revolution-
ary war versus an M16 rifle.

Once you qualify for a process such as ISO 9002,
people don't want you improving. That standard work
stuff reminds me of Ball State University as an under-
graduate. They had beautiful shrubbery and flowers,
but the sidewalks were squared. People cut across

the corners and tear out the bushes and flowers. They look ugly. So, finally they come in, ripped up all the sidewalks, and left it. Then put concrete over the cow paths. The bushes never got messed up. That was a $2-million savings.

We still walk around the same sidewalks and unfortunately fail to reinvent ourselves as an industry. We are the most innovative industry in terms of quality. (He is talking about quality.) There have been no other inventions in quality since Six Sigma. DMAIC is it. The D and the C are bookends to what is needed. The main point is this. Our industry needs to look upward toward the business floors of the corporation. That is where help is needed. We have had many years looking at process control, and tons of consultants, and nothing is helping businesses improve quality. A question to each executive is if he or she is in the business of quality. Are you leading them getting into the business of quality, are you concerned about the quality of your business, or are you trying to get into the business of quality? Does little good to have a Six Sigma part in a three-sigma business. We have to look toward making businesses Six Sigma. For example, from a business perspective, take the three determinants of customer satisfaction: highest quality, shortest time, and lowest cost. Separate quality; then it is design processes and capability. Control capability and complexity. We just kick it up a notch to the business level. We have business-related projects like improving the net present value (NPV). Most engineers would ask what internal rate of return (IRR) is. The current cost of capital. Engineers ask what that has to do with what I do. They fail to understand the hipbone, which is connected to the leg bone, and oscillations in the toe wind up as oscillation in the head. Getting to C is business terraforming, not business transformation. Creating a new environment on a dead planet. Changing one from being oxygen dependent to being carbon dependent. Transforming a business is not as good a fit to the business ecosystem. Within the ecosystem of the business, we have customers and suppliers and need a balance. Benchmark-dating healthcare handle bags better than our body. The 6.2 sigma is 1800 times better than our bags getting there. We don't look at our business as an ecosystem. Everything has to be more organic. In our leadership, we are a corporation, and that allows us to have great flexibility to improvise and adapt. The market has an ecosystem. When the two ecosystems cross paths, if they are not in sync, such as sharks in a koi pond, that is not a good deal. Think in terms of a business system, not independent unattached components.

Healthcare—let me start by saying this: "The healthcare business is no different from making automobiles." Y is a function of x. When you can define, measure, and analyze the Y, and diagnose, improve, and control the xs, physics will win every time. It's just that simple. When you try to short-circuit that system, you can stick your head in the sand. You cannot measure and say that it doesn't exist… or you can start measuring the things that are important to society and then take action. The waste that occurs in hospitals is appalling—not just material waste but also human waste in terms of productivity. Arrogant physicians are working like a machine and patients are parts to process. They think that they are independent entities who can send their surrogate doctors (nurse practitioners, physician assistants, nurses), which is really irritating when it is primarily to increase his income. He puts his profit on top and charges us for his time. We get lower care than what we paid for. We are not speaking to the people whom we want to pay. One doctor did not know anything about me. He was a surrogate of my primary doctor, and I told him to get out. My buddy wanted to change his provider.

The first place Mikel would start if he ran a hospital level is the eradication of fear. We measure the human beings so much and the business so little. The percentage of hospital executives who know their defects per unit would be less than 5%. The executive ranks need good education. They are unaware of how much the problem is costing them. They need to know how much bad quality costs them. Then, they will ask how we are going to get a handle on it. Start benchmarking around the sigmas of various businesses. Then, ask where we are when they see a chart of sigma level by business. First, understand where their current position is relative to the world of other businesses. How good are they compared to running restaurants and making cars? The first Pareto down is the next step. Now, hit them with the cost of poor quality. How big that number is for them. Pull out their accounting books. Then, they say, "Oh my God, are you kidding me?" Let me understand this. If you can capture 10% of this into education in the first wave, you will become more educated, and eradicate fear, and then we follow that with actual training what would this bring to the bottom line? If they correlated their patient experience with their financials, it is very strong. It starts to break down a little bit when it is in a system. Insurance is also a factor. Insurance as a covariant; there is high correlation.

In terms of healthcare, any attempt at the process level is taking a nickel off the national debt. Board members don't even know that they are undergoing Six Sigma training. Not a lot of fanfare at the top, and that is bad. More fanfare about a magnetic resonance imaging (MRI) because it is a big piece of capital equipment. He also runs into the CEOs who are made up of 1500 independents. I can't tell them what to do. There is a way to tackle this. Fix one hospital, and then have a standard presentation to visit the hospitals and see the quality. He would start with top leadership and educate them about reliability and how quality connects to the financial health of this healthcare organization. When a business administrator sees that, then how do I get at that? First thing to do is to eradicate fear of the people to expose their issues with a chart of their data and the consequences. That really tells us if he or she fears numbers. What consequence to the doctor if a test turns positive; they say that we will ssure you as much as we can.

I would like to deliver the same message that I heard 30 years ago—the exact same message. Start with understanding Six Sigma. 2. Eradicate fear. What is it going to take to move that? They need to understand what we are talking about and second, remove the fear factor. Third, educate people. Fourth, create strategic plans to use an improvement initiative that is correlated to the financial system and regain control of the core processes of that business. Then, the job will be faster and easier. Got to start with the doctor, and don't hire consultants to fix processes and the back room.

Start teaching quality programs in medical school. Teach nurses, too. Nurses see it going on every day. It doesn't take too many nights in a hospital to see and experience healthcare's lack of reliability. I have to commend you on writing this book on healthcare. Reliability is needed far more in this society, in our society. One last question for your readers, "What is your management reliability?"

Healthcare Leaders in Driving Higher Reliability

I have mentioned Mark Chassin, MD, and CEO of The Joint Commission, Brent James, MD, and chief quality officer of Intermountain Health, and others, and yet none of these organizations claim to have accomplished becoming an HRO. So, let us highlight organizations that show acceleration toward higher reliability. These healthcare professionals are the people to watch.

CHRISTUS[3] executives set forth a process to achieve higher reliability through clinical integration performance improvement. Several of their successes in achieving high reliability are shared in this book. They admit that CHRISTUS has a lot of work to do, but their early start is demonstrating results in some of its 20 sites in the initiative that they call clinical integration. Just the name of it sounds like they have Deming's focus on the system. Clinical integration sounds like something that HROs have. Executives at CHRISTUS are beginning their journey across its 20 sites internationally are making the right moves to start their journey. Time will tell if they can achieve high reliability.

The American Hospital Association defines clinical integration as such: "In essence, clinical integration involves providers working together in an interdependent fashion so that they can pool infrastructure and resources, and develop, implement and monitor protocols, 'best practices,' and various other organized processes that can enable them to furnish higher quality care in a more efficient manner than they likely could achieve working independently. Such programs can enable primary care physicians and specialists of all kinds to work more closely with each other in a coordinated fashion" (p. 5).[4]

Care that is safe was the focus of our work with CHRISTUS. We began clinical process of care measures that are evidence-based measures, which improve patient safety. Blood glucose management with patients who have undergone cardiac

surgery has proven to reduce the risk of surgical site infections, making it easier to identify patients who are diagnosed
with congestive heart failure (CHF) and better prepare them
for care after discharge, made the reliability of the CHF patient
care better. The better reliability also reduced readmissions
and the pain of CHF. We also reduced the length of stay at
some sites, and healthcare knows that the longer a patient is
in our care, the more likely are healthcare-acquired conditions. Thus, minimizing the length of stay once prepared for
the next level of care improves the reliability of outcomes and
safety.

Jayne Pope, CEO, Hill Country Memorial, and her team
won the Malcolm Baldrige Award, and we have seen in
Chapter 3 of this book their accomplishments and focus on
the patients and their staff.

And, Circle Partners may be a high-reliability healthcare
rising star in the United Kingdom. Steve Melton, CEO, and
Ahmed Mujtaba, the head of leadership development, share
with me annually their progress in implementing high-reliability
principles such as stop the line and team problem solving
using Lean, Six Sigma, Change Leadership, and Reliability in
its Circle Academy. Circle's focus is on patients, and they are
building internal capability in high-reliability skills. Circle's
principles include, "We measure everything we do." Circle
operates National Health Service acute care hospitals and
other healthcare sites and competes on quality and reliability.

Circle's Principles[5]

- *We are above all the agents of our patients.* We aim to
  exceed their expectations every time so that we earn their
  trust and loyalty. We strive to continuously improve the
  quality and value of the care that we give to our patients.
- *We empower our people to do their best.* Our people are our
  greatest asset. We should select them attentively and invest
  in them passionately. As everyone matters, everyone who

contributes should be a partner in all that we do. In return, we expect them to give their patients all that they can.

■ *We are unrelenting in the pursuit of excellence.* We embrace innovation and learn from our mistakes. We measure everything we do, and we share the data with all to judge. Pursuing our ambition to be the best healthcare provider is a never-ending process. *Good enough* never is.

There are many others in healthcare today who are achieving what these organizations have achieved and perhaps made better in some ways. I invite them to share their stories in achieving higher reliability on my website and blog. Shared learning is what accelerated Japan to achieve higher reliability in many products compared to the rest of the world. Deming was a big part of this sharing as he taught and coached leaders after World War II. We see the same successes across the globe when organizations share practices of reliability.

References

1. Excerpt from: W. Edwards Deming. 2012. *The Essential Deming: Leadership Principles from the Father of Quality.* Joyce Orsini and Diana Deming Cahill (Eds.). New York: McGraw-Hill Education. iBooks.
2. Interview Mikel Harry. April 2015 and http://www.mikeljharry.com/story.php?cid=8.
3. Gene Woods, Sherry Tichenor, Tom Diller, MD, Lillee Gelinas, and John Gillean, MD.
4. American Hospital Association. 2007. Guidance for Clinical Integration, a Working Paper Prepared for AHA by Hogan & Hartson, LLP. Available at http://www.aha.org/advocacy-issues/clininteg/index.shtml.
5. Available at http://www.circlehealth.co.uk/about-circle/our-credo#sthash.QTAGZdOD.pdf.

Chapter 10

Capability

Capability: The Precursor to Reliability

> Leaders: Capability is the competitive weapon for healthcare.

I would use these methods to achieve and compare my capabilities and reliability as a competitive weapon. I would be the only healthcare institution that is able to state capability, and I could set the bar. If other healthcare institutions feel that these are complex, that is in my favor too. This is called a barrier to entry. Higher reliability gained through capability provides value to the Centers for Medicare & Medicaid Services (CMS); the National Health Service in the United Kingdom; major payers such as Blue Cross Blue Shield and Bupa; and major corporations including Caterpillar, Ford, Toyota, Walmart, TESCO, and, most importantly, to us and our loved ones as patients. This is a barrier because very few healthcare organizations are using capability as described in this book resulting in reliability. No one else is prepared to provide such a competitive advantage.

I will cover capability by compartmentalizing the study of capability to make it easier to understand. The compartments are the following:

- Explain what capability means in terms of *the voice of the process* versus *the voice of the customer*
- Explain why capability is important in assessing reliability
- Explain the characteristics of a capability study
- Explain capability using statistical process control (SPC)
- Explain capability for continuous and attribute data

Capability is one-half of achieving reliability, as defined. Time is the second element in reliability, and is significant, but capability is the more important half and one that unfortunately differentiates healthcare from high-reliability organizations (HROs). One would not think of *not* doing the capability analyses that I share in this chapter in automotive, aerospace, electrical safety, aviation, and consumer electronics. I imagine that capability studies are done in making children's toys to ensure that they are capable for the expected time in function as well as safe. Think of a tricycle. What would happen if the tubular steel was too thin to support a child's weight and collapsed? The capability analysis with continuous data and high granularity would be what I would require in manufacturing the tricycles.

The Voice of the Customer

Reliability is defined in part by the person benefitting from the service or product and the person designing and providing the service or product. The patients in healthcare expect a better outcome from a surgical procedure than a worse outcome. I do not know of any patient who goes into surgery expecting to be worse off in total than not. How long the effects of the surgery occur is another element of the reliability of the surgery.

For a total knee replacement, the patients expect to be walking better and with less pain for many years. To have a total knee replacement that does not improve the patient's ambulatory ability and/or a replacement that fails requiring a readmission days after surgery is to have failed reliability. Healthcare often has to be the voice of the patients in highly complex processes where imaging, rehabilitation, pharmacological solutions, and social work are needed. The physicians take the responsibility to voice these needs for their patients. This is not uncommon in other industries, but I think that the providers in healthcare perform this voicing more.

Having physicians, nurses, and other staff as patients routinely improves the reliability of an organization. Healthcare can benefit in knowing the voice of the customer because almost all of us will become patients someday and be able to witness the reliability, or lack of, firsthand. This is not always true such as in my first company, which manufactures electrical safety products. Other than a homeowner or tenant occasionally switching back on a circuit breaker that tripped, very few circuit breakers ever fail, and thus many of our employees never experience installing or experiencing a failure. Thus, our engineers and electrical contractors became the major voice of the customer. Ease of designing a circuit breaker installation and installing are very important qualities and are often differentiators in selling. Thus, contractors are also customers, and reliability is very much stated in their contracts with us.

Leaders: Consider becoming the voice of your patients and staff. Experience firsthand your patients' and staff members' experiences, and report back to the staff your experience.

Use your authority to allow teams to gather and improve the experience using methods in this book. Above all, allow them to also gather the voice of the customer and empower them to act now to improve the reliability and experience.

Process Control and Capability

Many people are confused about process control and process capability. First of all, reliability in healthcare needs to focus on the voice of the patient. The patients care most about outcome reliability, not process capability. Using the equation, Y is a function of the xs, or simply, the outcome is based on the process inputs, which are denoted as xs. The patients want reliable outcomes. When they go in for interventional cardiology, they measure reliability by how they feel for a given time knowing that the vessel flow may eventually reduce again but after the expected time.

To get the reliable outcome that the patients expect, the cardiologist and the team must have a capable process. A capable process is one thing. Process performance is another. The patients are more concerned with process performance—getting the Y that they expect (performance to their specifications) over the amount of time that is expected rather than a process that is stable and capable. When we discuss high reliability, we are talking about the reliability of performance to the customer's specifications. Capable and stable processes get us the reliability with designs that allow reliability. Throughout this book, we will increase the knowledge of the contribution of design and process in achieving high reliability.

For services, we will discuss methods to assess the capability of two people making the correct judgment. I have a lot of respect for cardiologists and radiologists. I have seen hundreds of interventional cardiology procedures. In the catheterization laboratory, in a routine procedure to place a stent, the cardiologist inserts a wire into the arteries using fluoroscopy guidance. He or she looks for blockage in the vessel and places a stent to restore blood flow. It amazes me what the cardiologist and the catheterization laboratory team see as the area of concern. I could not pick out what they were seeing, and when I began to see, the next decision is how bad the blockage was and if a stent would be the best procedure. Judgment and use of appropriate Food and Drug Administration–approved technology, to determine if a stent should or should not be placed, define a great cardiologist.

Assessing the capability of a cardiologist in deciding if a stent is appropriate can be achieved using *attribute agreement analysis.*

Regardless of the industry, task, or whether performed by a human or machine, capability analysis is tremendously beneficial in achieving higher reliability. In fact, without knowing how to perform capability studies, one cannot assess reliability. This chapter differentiates HROs from those that do not perform capability analyses. Standard work is not needed nearly as much as capability is needed. The next time you hear someone say that the answer is standard work, demand that they prove capability to you first.

Every patient wants capable healthcare.
    Patients do not care if it is standardized until it is capable.

In fact, standardized work is by definition the most capable. Until we see these types of capability analyses in healthcare, we would not achieve high reliability. And yes, these same capability analyses are used to improve safety in HROs. So, consultants who propose achieving high reliability without ensuring capable and stable processes are not understanding the science behind HRO performance. HROs have all three: (1) capability, (2) culture for reliability, and (3) leadership knowledgeable about what it takes to achieve reliability.

There is not necessarily a time element with some definitions of capability, which is shared in the following paragraph. Understanding capability first and then applying the time element may make it simpler to truly appreciate reliability.

Equation 10.1 is well known in healthcare where Six Sigma has been deployed. Even though the equation is not a creation of Six Sigma, it is used universally to describe that outcomes are capable if the process variables are also capable. Outcomes are a function of inputs

$$Y = f(x_1, x_2 \ldots x_n) \qquad (10.1)$$

Where Y is the outcome, and xs are the input variables in the process that determine the level of the Y. The level of the Y desired is capability. Said another way, Y is the function of the xs. When Y is at the level that is desired, we have capability. Stabilize and control the xs to achieve the acceptable Ys = capability.

The capability measured, and therefore reliability, is affected by

- Process variation
- Process off center of customer tolerance range
- Supplier variation
- Arbitrary and restrictive process specifications (tighter than the customers require)
- Demand variation
- Measurement system variation (Blood pressure reading varies from caregiver to caregiver.)

How capable we need to be may be determined by

- Your patient
- Your cost goals
- Technology limits
- Competitive advantage
- Supplier's capability

In processes that are very erratic and one cannot predict well the outcome, the first task may be to achieve stability and then work to improve capability.

Capability Case Study

A team at CHRISTUS wanted to improve its patient experience survey results. CMS in October 2012 started incentivizing over 3000 acute care hospitals in the United States to achieve above-average performance in patient experience, as well as clinical process of care measures such as managing the urinary catheter removal in a timely manner, which is proven to reduce the risk of infection. I add that there are penalties, too, for hospitals that fall below the national average.

CHRISTUS Santa Rosa had three hospitals, all in the penalty box, and wanted quick improvement that sustained to moving from a penalty that reduced every dollar of Medicare reimbursement to an organization that achieved more reimbursement than breakeven. The team learned my high-reliability roadmap and chartered the effort. This included being very clear on what was required by CMS and how capable the team was expected to be to call this a success.

The next steps were to identify the stakeholders who are affected by this project, which includes the patients, the surgeons, the nurses, and all those who are affected when infections result from poor catheter management. The next step is always critical in capability analysis—measuring the current state of performance. In capability analysis, this means determining the current capability of complying with CMS' requirement of 100% compliance. In Figure 10.1, we see a graphical and statistical capability analysis of managing the catheters at the start of the project.

The histogram shows the percentage of compliance in removing or documenting a physician's reason to not remove the urinary catheter. One hundred percent (100%) is perfect,

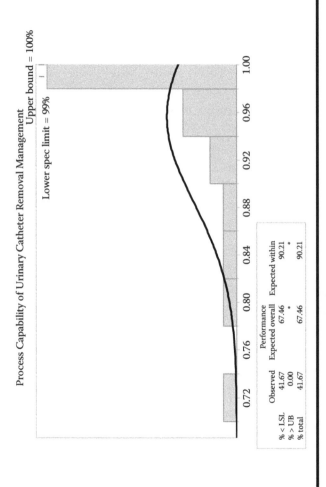

Figure 10.1 Capability of complying with CMS' Urinary Catheter Management Specification (SCIP-9).

meaning that every catheter inserted was managed to CMS' specifications. Anything less than 100% is failure. The team initially chartered a goal to achieve 99% and later achieve a high reliability of 100% for at least a year.

The team had periods of compliance in the 70% range. This process is not capable as judged by many healthcare organizations that have achieved 100% compliance for years. Note the statistic of 67.46%. This is the expected percentage compliance over the long run if the hospitals do not improve. In other words, the hospitals only met their goal of 99% 33% of the time (100% − 67.46% = 32.54%).

In the voice of the patient, the hospitals failed nearly two-thirds of its patients—not capable. That is why CHRISTUS scored much higher than many in the nation yet was still not satisfied until 100% high reliability was achieved and set out to use Six Sigma and achieve its goal. After applying the high-reliability roadmap, all three hospitals achieved over one year of perfect compliance—two of the hospitals achieved zero defects from the first week of work.

Christie Paulsen, a Baylor resident, led the regional effort with Angie Lambert, Elsie Graves, and Deon Hobbs serving as project champions and all the chief nursing officers of their hospitals. Patty Toney, the chief nursing executive of the region, and these three hospitals served them as executive sponsor and keep on supporting the teams as they continue to improve urinary catheter management. Sherry Tichenor, the chief quality officer of the entire CHRISTUS system, appreciated their success; she suggested that every 1 of the 20 hospitals should learn from CHRISTUS Santa Rosa and expect the same high reliability.

Performing Capability Analyses

There are many methods to measure capability, and healthcare has only begun to start measuring capability using these methods that are required by Ford, GM, Chrysler, and similar requirements that Toyota, Nissan, and Subaru demand. We will use Minitab, a popular statistical software program both inside and outside healthcare.

Leaders: Consider investing in one of your staff who is passionate about achieving high reliability by ensuring that he or she has the resources to apply the methods in this book.

Achieving high reliability demands a data-driven culture and performance improvement in addition to the softer cultural and behavioral skills. With software, the statistics part is the easier part in achieving high reliability. Allow your high-reliability leaders to focus on the human factors more than the statistics.

There are many ways to measure capability, and the most popular measures include sigma. In the example in Table 10.1, we see a popular use of sigma to measure the capability of well-known processes.

As the sigma level increases, yield also increases, which translates to improved capability. The customers should determine the yield that is desired for the price that they are willing to pay.

Table 10.1 Capability Chart for Various Levels of Quality

Sigma Level	Defects-per-Million Opportunities	Yield Percentage
1	690,000	<50
2	308,537	69.1
3	66,807	93.32
4	6210	99.379
5	233	99.9767
6	3.4	99.99966

Another measure of capability is defects per million. In Table 10.1, one can see a direct correlation between sigma level, yield, and defects-per-million opportunities. Any of these measures of capability are useful.

Capability Analysis of Continuous Data with High Granularity

Figure 10.2a and b shows the graphical and statistical analyses of capability in responding to a patient's request for help.

The voice of the patient suggests a response should come within 2 minutes (120 seconds). Also, the team is aware that patients inadvertently press the call button and, if recognized, will cancel the alarm. The upper specification limit of 120 seconds can be graphically displayed as a vertical line at 120 seconds. We could add a lower specification for inadvertent call light alarms, say, at 20 seconds, to show *not* to respond immediately as the patient or advocate cancels the false alarm.

The graphical and statistical analysis from Minitab's Assistant feature quickly shows that only 98% of the observed data shows that the team responded within 120 seconds (2% defective is the percentage of times above the 120 seconds specification range), which suggests that the team is capable most of the time in responding within the time that is desired. About 17,000 times out of 1 million, we would expect to fail. We do not know how this represents the process day in and day out nor at different times in the day, such as during the very busy morning shift change.

Knowing the duration of time that the team is capable of responding within 120 seconds would be our next step in understanding the reliability of responding to patient requests for help. This time element that is missing will complete the measurement of reliability. But, let us stay with measuring and understanding capability in this chapter. I will explain more of the output on this chart in this chapter as we learn the measures of capability.

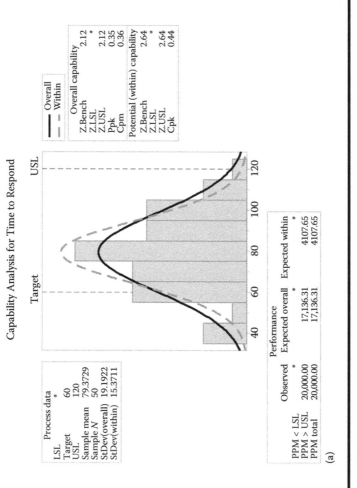

Figure 10.2 **(a) Capability in responding to patient requests for help with Six Sigma Program commonly used statistics.**

(Continued)

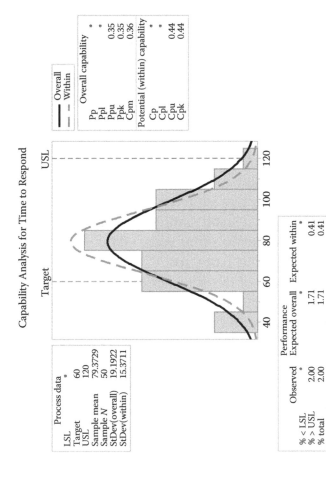

Capability Analysis for Time to Respond

Process data	
LSL	*
Target	60
USL	120
Sample mean	79.3729
Sample N	50
StDev(overall)	19.1922
StDev(within)	15.3711

		Performance	
	Observed	Expected overall	Expected within
% < LSL	*	*	*
% > USL	2.00	1.71	0.41
% total	2.00	1.71	0.41

— Overall
-- Within

Overall capability	
Pp	*
Ppl	*
Ppu	0.35
Ppk	0.35
Cpm	0.36

Potential (within) capability	
Cp	*
Cpl	*
Cpu	0.44
Cpk	0.44

(b)

Figure 10.2 (Continued)   (b) Capability in responding to patient requests for help with Cpk; Ppk capability statistics required in some automotive applications.

The sigma level of the response time found in Figure 10.2a is the Z.Bench overall statistic. The sigma level of this process is 2.12 or about 2 sigma using Minitab. There is an adjustment made called a 1.5 sigma shift that was derived empirically by Motorola that accounts for a shifting of the center of process performance.

In Figure 10.2b, we see other capability statistics with the same data. In the automotive industry, another popular measure of capability is what Ford, GM, Chrysler, and many other customers require of suppliers and their own organizations. Ford, GM, Chrysler, Eaton, SKF, United Airlines, and thousands of other companies use capability as I demonstrate here. Toyota, too, requires a capability analysis that is similar to these examples.

In 2004, when I was the head of quality for SKF Seals USA, we would perform capability for all our automotive customers, but for Toyota, they were more interested in the graphical capability histogram and a small sample than in the capability statistics that I showed. Realize that Ford, GM, and Chrysler required the histogram and parts, too.

Cpk and Ppk are two of the statistics that are recognized in the automotive industry and often required to sell to Ford, GM, or Chrysler. The Cpk in the response example 9 (Figure 10.2b) is 0.44. The Cpk required is often 1.33 or higher. Thus, this process may not be capable. The Ppk is 0.35 and is the preferred statistic for some organizations because it represents the probability of capability better over the long term.

Healthcare will benefit from capability indices like Cp and Pp, Cpk, and Ppk and plotting the distribution that the process delivers with the customer specifications that are graphically depicted on the histogram.

A brief overview of the most popular indices is covered here. I prefer the Cpk and Ppk over the Cp and Pp because the prior indices provide a statistic of variation and centering, not just variation. Think of the football analogy. A tight distribution of kicks is good but entirely not capable if all the footballs fall outside of the goal posts. The Cpk and Ppk describe how centered the process is, too.

Bilateral and Unilateral Tolerances (Specifications)

A bilateral tolerance is used to measure capability when dissatisfaction can occur if too high and too low. Think of blood glucose control. Too low or too high is not healthy for the patient. This specification is called a bilateral tolerance or specification. In emergency department (ED) wait times, I do not think that anyone would complain of being seen really quickly. For ED wait times and wait times across healthcare, we usually are concerned with only one side of the process distribution—times that are too long. Being concerned with only the left or right side of a distribution is an example of a unilateral or one-sided tolerance or specification.

Capability Indices

Let us cover the most popular and often required capability statistics that are used in automotive,[1] aerospace, electrical safety, and many other industries. Remember that stability comes before capability. These indices are only valid if the process is in SPC. Check the process output over time using the appropriate SPC chart before using these indices.

Processes are often not stable, and defects may occur. Do not be misled by some who say that one has to bring the process under control first. That does not make sense, especially if rapid improvement is needed such as in medical emergencies. Get the process resulting in the least amount of failures, and then stabilize it. Finally, consider one of these indices if your data are of continuous type and you need this level of granularity. And, remember that every process that becomes stable and is capable is a candidate for continuous improvement and a new level of performance.

Do not be misled that the goal is standard work. No, the goal is continuously improving reliability and achieving temporary stability and standard work reflecting the new improved ways. Patients do not give a darn about standard work. We care about capability over time being equal to reliability.

Cp

Cp is a capability index that measures the capability of the process in meeting the variability requirements. Using blood glucose as an example, this statistic could help caregivers assess how well they can control blood glucose levels. The higher the Cp value, the better the capability. Today, we could use this statistic or one of the capability indices following to choose the better protocol for blood glucose management. I think that it helps us understand this and the other indices if we understand how they are calculated. Do not worry about memorizing these because the software does it all for us. I just want all readers to understand what the Cp tells us and what it does not, so we can choose the best capability index. We take the upper specification limit and subtract the lower specification limit in the numerator. This gives us the tolerance range or spread that is allowed by the customer. We divide this by the spread of the actual process using six times the population standard deviation. Six times the standard deviation estimates 99% of the values. Thus, a Cp of 1.00 suggests that 99% of the process output is within the tolerance range allowed.

$$Cp = \frac{USL - LSL}{6\sigma_c} \tag{10.2}$$

Graphically, it might look like Figure 10.3a or b.

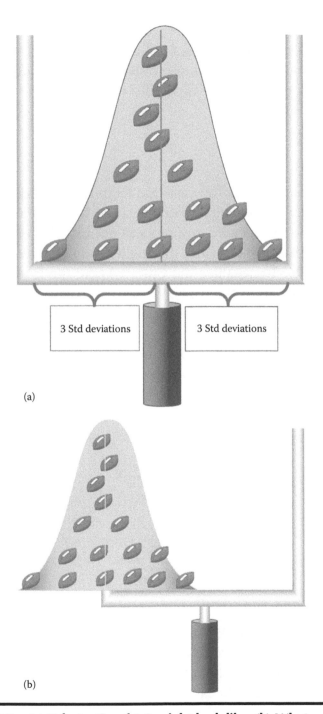

(a)

(b)

Figure 10.3   (a) What a Cp of 1.0 might look like. (b) What a Cp of 1.0 might also look like.

Have you noticed the difference between Figure 10.3a and b? The same distribution of data from a process can have the exact same spread. But, the centering of the process is different, and we realize clearly that the capability of spread alone may not be enough to compete.

Cpk

Cpk accounts for both the variation as in the Cp index and the centering. For bilateral tolerances, the Cpk will always be less than the Cp because any process not exactly centered will decrease this statistic. Again, the higher the Cpk, the higher the capability. To calculate the Cpk, we take the lower of the Cpu and Cpl. Cpu is the capability index using the upper specification limit and Cpl for the lower. The lowest (worst capability) of the two is the more conservative estimate of the process capability and thus the one that we use for Cpk. $\overline{X}$ is the mean of the subgroup averages. Samples are taken of the process output and averaged. The average of those means is pronounced as *x double bar.*

$$Cpu = \frac{USL - \overline{\overline{X}}}{3\sigma_c} \tag{10.3}$$

$$Cpl = \frac{\overline{\overline{X}} - LSL}{3\sigma_c} \tag{10.4}$$

Using Figure 10.3b, Equation 10.3 would have a higher value than Equation 10.4 because the distribution is much closer to the lower specification limit than the upper. Thus, we must choose Equation 10.4 because it is the more conservative value for the Cpk.

The Cpk is the more popular capability index when a bilateral specification is given.

Leaders: Simply asking for the Cpk statistic and supporting your staff in calculating it for issues where variability is a concern will help healthcare improve reliability.

That is why Ford, GM, and Chrysler require this or similar capability statistics before production begins. At times, the capability or stability is not achieved, so sorting out defective parts or services is required. This is waste and is not the outcome that is desired for the long term.

Pp

This capability statistic is called the performance index because it compares the process using the overall standard deviation. The Pp uses the within-subgroup variation. Think of it this way. The Cpk considers only the variation within the samples that are used to calculate the variance. The Ppk uses the between-subgroup variation as well as the within-subgroup variation. Thus, it is usually more conservative to state the capability of a process using the Pp and Ppk statistics rather than the Cp and Cpk. For more on the standard deviation differences and within- and between-subgroup variation, see my website, Minitab help, or the Automotive Industry Action Group (AIAG) Manual[1] or search online.

$$Pp = \frac{USL - LSL}{6\sigma_p} \qquad (10.5)$$

$$Ppl = \frac{\overline{X} - LSL}{3\sigma_p} \qquad (10.6)$$

$$Ppl = \frac{USL - \overline{X}}{3\sigma_p} \qquad (10.7)$$

Both the Cp and the Cpk should be considered together. If the Cp is much greater than the Cpk, then the process has centering opportunities. The same goes for the Pp and Ppk.

Each index has a capability ratio. The CR and PR are simply the reciprocals of Cp and Pp, respectively. These are meaningless for unilateral tolerances.

Okay. Now that you know the most required capability indices, I will take you step by step through a capability analysis. These steps are used regardless of which index you choose.

Six Steps to Calculate Capability with Continuous Data and Need for Higher Granularity

The steps are as follows:

1. The voice of the customer's specification limits.
2. Validate the measurement system.
3. The voice of the process data collection represents the process.
4. Distribution analysis and data integrity.
5. Plot process stability.
6. Calculate process capability.

Healthcare has many examples of a capability study that is beneficial when the data are of continuous type, and the need is for high granularity. The value of continuous data again shows in assessing capability. We can use powerful analytical techniques that are more precise to know that we have achieved capability for a short time. And, we can use the more powerful SPC charts to understand over time how the process is performing. Continuous data measured in real time with SPC allow us to act to prevent failure well in advance of losing the capability.

Step 1: The Voice of the Customer's Specification Limits

The voice of the customer is the most important task in a capability analysis because capability is defined as performance to the customer's specifications. The time to respond to a patient's call light is a valuable application of continuous data with high granularity because the patient's expectations are to have a response within minutes versus hours and days.

Step 2: Ensuring That Your Measurement System Is Capable of Measuring Capability

Too often, healthcare decisions are made on data that are not correct. I shared a healthcare organization's quality scores recently, and the CEO exclaimed that he had no idea that their clinical safety scores were as poor as the publicly available data that I had. As most of you know, CMS data comes from the organization itself. However, in counting the readmissions of any one organization, CMS' count may be higher because CMS knows of patients who are readmitted at facilities other than the original admission hospital. CMS includes these additional readmissions in the count of readmissions that are known to the original admitting hospital.

Although the difference, bias, is usually small, it demonstrates a flaw in the measurement system that cannot account for all readmissions. We call this error a bias because CMS will have more readmissions than the original admitting hospital, not less. We can calculate the bias with enough data and better estimate the total readmissions. I do not want readers thinking that measuring readmissions is hopeless. An HRO will find a measurement system that works well enough despite the hardships.

Another flawed measurement system is in judging healthcare-acquired conditions. I have witnessed very experienced physicians and epidemiologists debating what is, and what is not, an infection. The moral of these healthcare measurement system stories is that reliability is dependent on quality measurements. Step 2 is critical before claiming capability, and do not let teams skip it. Ensuring an accurate and precise measurement system is absolutely necessary in a capability study. We must know truth in the data to say that we are capable.

For more information on how to measure the quality and improve a measurement system, refer to the AIAG manual[1] on measurement system analysis or Chapter 12 in my book *Utilizing the 3Ms of Process Improvement in Healthcare.*

First, let us understand what is meant by data type. This is critical in choosing the correct measurement system for your capability analysis.

Categories and Types of Data

Measurement system analysis techniques vary based on the categories of data and types of data that one wants in the measurement system. The categories are

- *Quantitative (numerical responses)*—variables that are numeric and often ordinal.
- *Qualitative (categorical responses)*—variables for which an attribute or classification is measured.

Quantitative (numerical responses)—
There are two types of data within the quantitative category:

1. *Continuous (variable data).* Any point on a histogram is possible such as when decimal subdivisions are possible:
   a. Data that indicate how much or how many.
      i. Variable data can be subdivided into finer increments of precision:
         A. Time (seconds)
         B. Speed (feet/minute)
         C. Rate (inches/time)
         D. Dimensions (millimeters)
2. *Discrete (attribute).* Numerical responses from a counting process where not every point is possible on a histogram:
   a. Good or bad counts
   b. Number of machines working
   c. Shifts of overtime scheduled
   d. Counted things (number of errors in a document, number of units shipped, etc.)
   e. Percentage of good or bad (percentage derived from counting)

Qualitative (categorical responses)—variables for which an attribute or classification is measured.
   – Yes or no
   – Good or bad
   – Meets the standard or does not

Continuous data are more desirable for most statistical analyses when small changes are valuable to know. Measuring if patient experiences are good or bad is viable and often done. If a scale is used, say, from 0 to 10 with 10 being excellent, more discrimination is possible, and an improvement team assessing if improvements are having an effect may be able to see changes sooner with the 0–10 scale.

We generally prefer continuous-type data, but we can also measure the capability of qualitative-type data that are also very common in healthcare. The statistical analysis known as *attribute agreement analysis* is very powerful in assessing the capability of people coming to the correct conclusion or judgment. We use this type of capability study in everything from how to judge sepsis to assessing the quality of care that is provided by two or more different providers or staff. In my first book, I covered attribute agreement analysis with a fun exercise measuring the capability of people judging the manufacturer of two different sodas.

Step 3: The Voice of the Process Data Collection Represents the Process

Step 3 is collecting data that will be used to assess how capable the process is in achieving the desired outcome. The equation

$$Y = f(x_1, x_2 \ldots x_n) \tag{10.8}$$

Is again useful in capability analysis. We are measuring the outcome, Y, to state the capability.

Step 4: Distribution Analysis and Data Integrity

Let us begin with understanding the shape of the data that we received by measuring the process outcome. There are three common shapes of data:

1. *Normally distributed data are commonly referred to as "bell shaped."* (See Figure 10.4.) Normally distributed data allow us to use the statistical capability techniques that are shared in this chapter directly without needing to transform non-normal data into normal data. All of the distributions I share here are also known as probability distributions. It is the probability statistic that we rely on to determine capability.
2. *Bimodal or distributions with more than one predominant, frequently occurring value.* An example is in

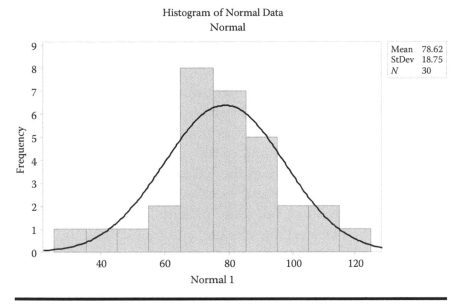

Figure 10.4   Normally distributed data.

Figure 10.5. The probability distribution or histogram shows two frequently occurring values separated by much lower values suggesting two modes. This shape is often a result of two different processes such as a process performed one way by one group, say, a shift, and a different way of performing on another shift. It can

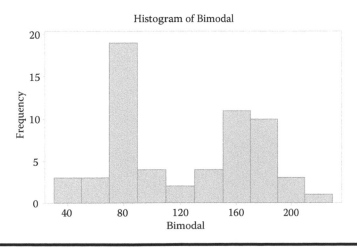

Figure 10.5   A bimodal distribution.

lead a high-reliability team quickly to the root causes and solutions by understanding what is different in the lower-performing group.

In Figure 10.6, we see a very common-shaped distribution because the measurement of time often follows this shape. This is a skewed distribution. The mode, the most frequently occurring value, is not in the middle of the distribution. The right tail of the distribution is spread farther from the mode than the left tail. Wait times to see a clinician follow this shape because the average wait time may be fairly short, but some patients may wait very long times, well beyond the average, and thus extend the right side of the distribution.

3. *Another skewed distribution is skewed the opposite way.* (See Figure 10.7.) In reliability, we often see this shape in the data. Early failures compared to the majority will be seen as skewing the distribution to the left. Examples in healthcare of this shape are wait times for interventional cardiology when a level 1 trauma ED shares the same catheterization laboratory with clinical office demand for cardiology procedures. The emergency patients will be

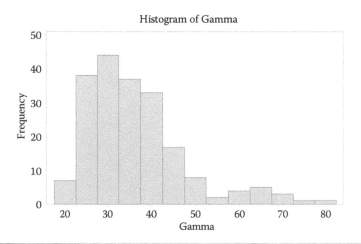

Figure 10.6   A right-skewed distribution.

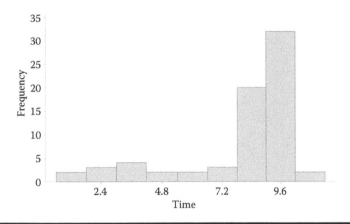

Figure 10.7   Histogram of left-skewed data.

treated much sooner than the higher volume of patients who are scheduled after a clinical visit with no emergency situation.

Step 5: Plot Process Stability

There is no guarantee of capability without achieving process stability. The leadership heard that the staff had responded in less than 4 minutes every day. Would you feel comfortable saying that this process is capable of meeting the goal of 4 minutes or less? While it is true that the SPC chart shows that at no time did the response take more than 4 minutes, what do you see that suggests that the 4-minute wait time might not be reliable? See Figure 10.8.

Doesn't it look like the times to respond are showing a trend higher and thus likely to exceed the goal of under 4 minutes? If we were to simply plot the data on a histogram, one could say that the process was capable of staying under 4 minutes. But, time is a factor in reliability and capability. We would not feel comfortable stating capability in this process of responding because the process is becoming unstable—it is changing. Who can say what the capability of responding is now as the times start increasing?

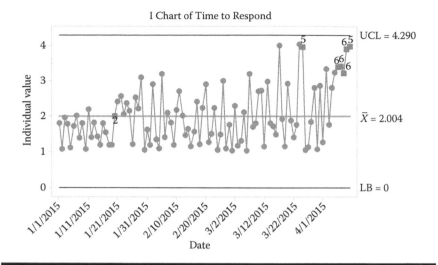

Figure 10.8   Time to respond.

The rule is always assess process stability in order to understand how your process behaves over time. Control charts are the recommended tool.

Step 6: Calculate Process Capability

Now, for the task we have waited, this is a statistically valid way to measure how capable we are to the customer's specifications. When healthcare starts performing these six steps and continuously improving, we will achieve our vision of healthcare becoming an HRO.

The concept of capability that Toyota, Ford, GM, and others used is the following concept.

In Figure 10.9, we see how a process's distribution of performance is compared to customer specifications. The histogram illustrates the process performance, and the two vertical lines illustrate the customer's specification limits. The histogram shows the process output (the voice of the process). The vertical lines are the specification limits of the customer (the voice of the customer). This process looks like it will result in performance well inside of the specification limits, so we

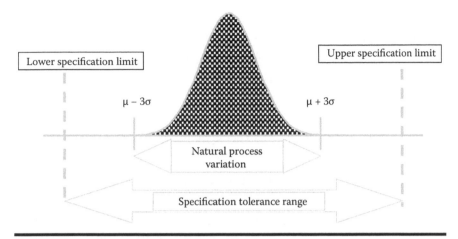

Lower specification limit

Upper specification limit

$\mu - 3\sigma$

$\mu + 3\sigma$

Natural process
variation

Specification tolerance range

Figure 10.9 Process performance and customer specification limits.

consider this process capable. If it performs this way through-out the expected time, we have reliability.

There are a number of ways to measure capability. The answer as to which method and statistic is used lies with the essence of measuring capability—satisfy your customers by using the methods and statistics that they wish. In healthcare, let us face it—the patients cannot always articulate what they want. A total hip replacement patient may not be able to spec-ify in medical acumen how much time he or she needs before he or she is able to drive a car again. This does not absolve us from searching for what the patients value, even if what they value is new to our expectations of what they *want*.

You have probably heard of asking the patients what they would like to achieve today, rather than the historically one-sided specification from healthcare telling the patients what we will do to them and what to expect. Although the patients may not know what to expect in capability specifications for treatment outcomes, any of them can answer the *specification* details for this type of question.

These six steps are the most popular capability analyses in automotive, aviation, aerospace, and electrical safety products and services. Whether we are reducing the time for staff to respond to a customer or making critical safety products, we use these same concepts and statistics. This is really quite easy using statistical software. The key is that we gain the confidence that we can state our capability accurately for our sake and our clients.

The three ways to describe data are basically how we assess capability. The shape of the distribution as noted in step 4 guides us in using the correct statistics of capability, the spread of the distribution relative to the specifications tells us how much margin, if any, the process has in delivering the outcome that is desired, and the central tendency is seen in the distribution. The central tendency is very important because processes shift over time, and if the spread is taking up most of the specification range, even small shifts will result in failures.

The spread and shifting of the process center are why Motorola worked to achieve a Six Sigma level of quality. Mikel Harry, in his interview with me shared in Chapter 9, goes into more detail.

Kicking a Goal and Capability: The Concept

The common analogy to understand spread, shift, and shape is football. This works for American football as well as what the rest of the world knows as football.

Imagine that we are teaching field goal kicking. The goal posts, vertical poles, are the specification limits much like the net area in soccer. We want to start out with the highest probability of kicking the ball between the goal posts, so exactly centered between the goal posts is ideal.

Looking at Figure 10.10, we see how the distribution of the kicking (the process output) can describe our capability in scoring. The shape is normal, bell shaped, which suggests that we have one kicking method most likely, and the symmetry of the normal distribution shows that we vary equally both left and right of the center. The spread of the kicking is evident. We have a lot of spread relative to the specifications because we observe kicks that are left and right of the specifications despite our kicks being centered. And, we just covered the

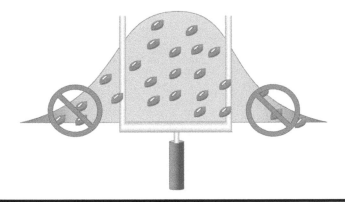

Figure 10.10   Poor capability with the football analogy.

centering. One can see that we would have even more failures if we were kicking left or right of center a majority of the time.

Bill Smith and Mikel Harry of Motorola shared with the world why achieving a Six Sigma level of quality was important for Motorola to compete. I use this same kicking analogy to describe a process that has achieved a Six Sigma level of quality. See Figure 10.11.

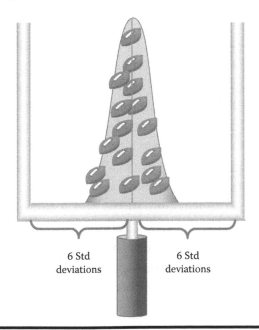

6 Std
deviations

6 Std
deviations

Figure 10.11   What a Six Sigma process looks like.

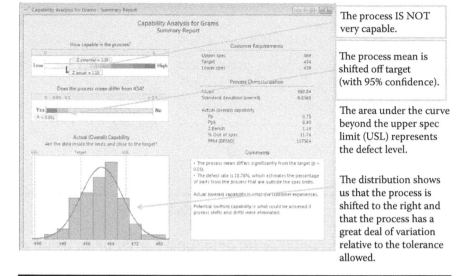

Figure 10.12 showing the Capability Analysis for Grams Summary Report with annotations:
- The process IS NOT very capable.
- The process mean is shifted off target (with 95% confidence).
- The area under the curve beyond the upper spec limit (USL) represents the defect level.
- The distribution shows us that the process is shifted to the right and that the process has a great deal of variation relative to the tolerance allowed.

Figure 10.12   Capability analysis of achieving 454 ± 15 grams.

Minitab's Assistant Feature in Capability Analysis*

Pharmacies need reliability in compounding processes to ensure that the right amount of each compound is used. Weighing and counting are two very common measurements in any pharmacy. Measuring the capability of weighing is critical. In the following example, we test the measurement system's capability in measuring the weight of a component. The nominal, or desired, weight is 454 grams. The tolerance allows the pharmacist to be plus or minus 15 grams. We use Minitab's Assistant feature to perform the capability analysis. See Figures 10.12 through 10.15. The Assistant automates much of the capability analysis, reducing time to select menu options. It also shares interpretation of the results.

In Figure 10.15, we see the capability analysis. HROs drive for capability and achieve it with controls to sustain capability.

---

* Minitab software version 17 with Assistant menu features.

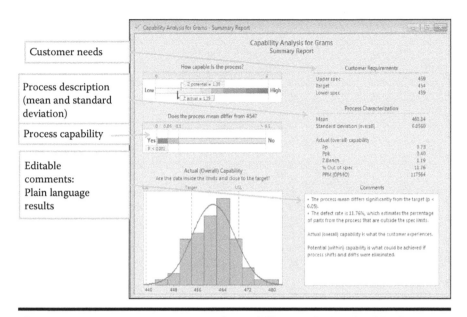

Figure 10.13   Summary report of capability analysis of achieving 454 ± 15 grams.

• Evaluates two key assumptions of capability analysis (normal): (1) Are the data stable? and
  (2) Do the data come from a normal distribution?

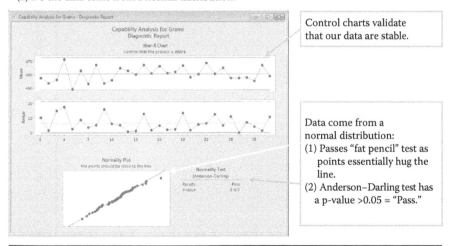

Figure 10.14   Diagnostic report of capability analysis of achieving 454 ± 15 grams.

The Details of Both Actual (Overall/Long-Term) and Potential (Within/Short-Term) Capabilities

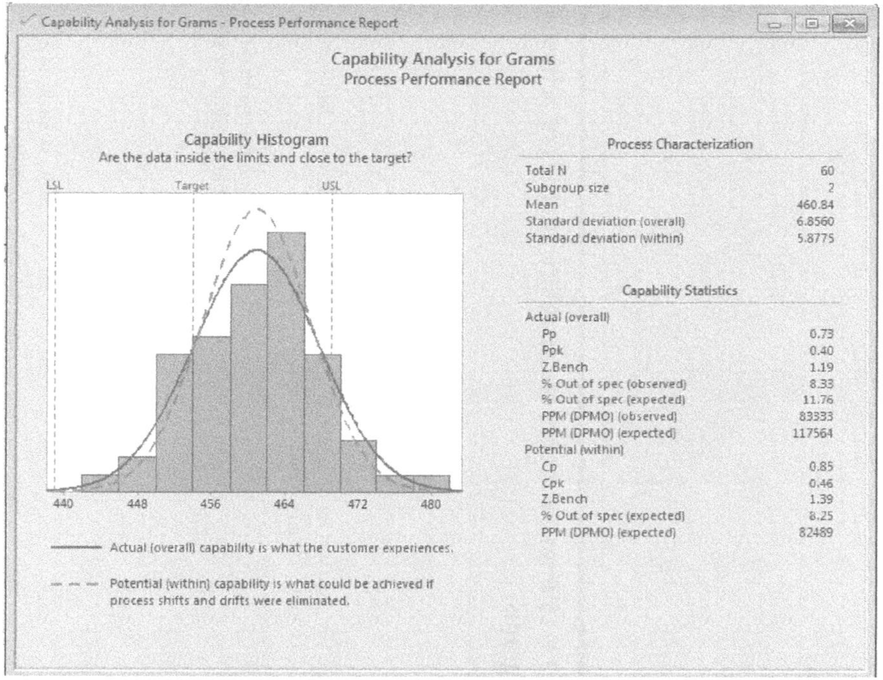

Figure 10.15 Process performance report of capability analysis.

Reference

1. DaimlerChrysler Corporation, Ford Motor Company, and General Motors. 2005. Statistical Process Control SPC, Second Edition. *Automotive Industry Action Group Reference Manual.* 1995.

Chapter 11

Design for Reliability— Products and Services

Unifying Instructive Force

Three automotive companies, specifically Ford, General Motors (GM), and Chrysler, collaborated to help the entire U.S. automotive industry improve quality. Much of the reliability learning comes from the Automotive Industry Action Group (AIAG) manuals.*

In healthcare, there has not emerged such a unifying force. We owe much to The Joint Commission (TJC) for pioneering and authoring many of the standards that are used today in virtually every hospital. CMS adopted its standards when Medicare was introduced, which makes its conditions of participation (CoPs) and TJC's standards very similar. They have grown to be more similar again after TJC was required to conform to the CoPs after the statute was eliminated allowing it accreditation rights by statute. I have grown appreciation for TJC's research and energy to create and share practices that improve quality.

---

* APQP, PPAP, and capability versus performance from AIAG SPC reference manuals.

Healthcare's lack of focus on capability has slowed its ascent to higher reliability. Overrelying on "We just need standard work" has also slowed our ascent. It is not standard work unless it is most capable. Everyone *jumping off the cliff* does not make jumping off the cliff the right thing to do.

This brings us to the focus in the automotive industry in achieving capability to the specifications. These companies united to create programs that design quality and help the suppliers achieve the capability that is desired in quality and capability in producing to meet the demand.

The first program that every supplier must learn and apply is advanced product quality planning (APQP). The purpose of APQP is to design in quality and have a fact-based and data-driven methodology to ensure quality at expected demand levels. Everyone knows how capability in terms of quality may be achieved in the first days of service and later fail when the demand increases. Toyota joins Ford, GM, and Chrysler in the application of APQP and essentially expects the same quality and capability and reporting on the firms that were formerly known as the Big Three.

One difference between the U.S. automakers and Toyota is the specific statistics that are required to be achieved in measuring capability. Ford, GM, and Chrysler required in my time in automotive achieving a Cpk and Ppk of specified levels, whereas Toyota focuses more on graphical evidence of capability and specifically histograms and actual parts that are made from the actual production equipment at demand volume.

Production Part Approval Process

Production part approval process (PPAP) is the second program that healthcare could greatly benefit from internally as well as with its suppliers and postdischarge partners. Population health can be explained as a system-wide look at health. Healthcare is moving away from an extreme acute care hospital mindset as ambulatory outpatient services replace acute care hospital stays. Yet, even an ambulatory surgical center needs to take a system-wide approach preparing patients well before the surgery to reduce the risk of infection by proper bathing, nutrition, and health. The ambulatory surgical center must also create a robust process for post surgical care including therapy, nutrition, and assisting post-care facilities such as Skilled Nursing Facilities in how to extend the healing.

PPAP comes after APQP and focuses on determining the actual capability and reliability of the service or product before full production for the customers. PPAP assures a level of quality before shipping production levels.

An example in healthcare is to have an electronic medical record system that actually works per specifications before launch. Included in the implementation would be a failure mode and effects analysis (FMEA) and control plan proving that the supplier actually thought through how the system might fail, controls to prevent failure, or at least detect failure to allow mitigation of the failure, and statistical process control (SPC) verification of the capability of the system. There would be key criteria with measures that are important to the customers who use the system. The customers include providers, nurses, therapists, and all who use the information directly or indirectly. Indirectly means the patients, advocates, and preadmit and postdischarge healthcare organizations such as clinics, skilled nursing facilities, long-term care hospitals, and organizations using its data to solve and prevent healthcare issues.

Population health strategies include using data to gain knowledge of the xs that affect our health. I will cover population health in Chapter 14. We have a massive untapped mine of data and value that is only now beginning to be recognized. Already, we can more quickly treat to reduce mortality from sepsis and assist surgeons in preparing patients for the most common procedure in the United States, a total knee replacement, with a handheld simple assessment with immediate feedback on the probability of readmission and treatment recommendations. These improvements are made possible by data and statistical analysis on finding the key drivers.

There are consultants who have promoted that analysis using statistics beyond a time series chart with perhaps a trend line or a Pareto chart is not needed in healthcare. This promotes false expectations and hinders healthcare's ability in becoming a high-reliability organization (HRO). HROs such as Eaton, SKF, and Motorola and Dr. Brent James with his work with data and analytics at Intermountain Healthcare not only have used the concepts in this book but also are required to do business in most of their markets.

Healthcare is using statistical analysis, and we use it in every major effort. At Intermountain, Dr. James teaches providers and staff to use data to find the root causes and prove the more effective treatments. He promotes statistical run charts that are simple but backed by statistical significance. He pushes for validating root causes and testing if solution ideas really work. Dr. James has been considered as one of the most likely people who can truly reform healthcare.

Consultants who make statements such as, "Healthcare does not need Six Sigma; it just needs Lean," or suggest that organizations should start with Lean because it is easier are misleading healthcare. These *Lean zealots* who define Lean as the simpler tools of productivity improvement and not quality improvement and who think that something as complex as healthcare can be solved by observing a few hours, or even days, and doing value stream maps and some 5S activities are one reason that healthcare is lagging behind HROs. These organizations, including Toyota, have gained knowledge and solutions from reliability engineering and analytics.

We use statistical analysis when we reduce readmissions, eliminate surgical site infections, and improve the survivability of patients with sepsis. How would you feel if Eaton did not use statistical analysis to know if the circuit breaker in your home will *trip* if the electrical current gets so high that the wires in your house will overheat and cause a fire? What if SKF did not use statistical methods in making the seals in your car allowing water to enter the bearings, overheat, and cause a *wheel off,* a catastrophic event in which a wheel detaches from the vehicle or remains on the vehicle and causes a fire due to the heat of friction at 70 miles per hour?

Getting back to healthcare, how would you feel if the drugs your doctors prescribed did not have an analysis validating an effect—and are not safe? Healthcare is advanced in research in statistical analysis. We need to take many of the same statistical methods and apply them to the front line in designing and running our healthcare processes. APQP is one of several standardized work methods that the automotive industry uses to ensure reliability.

APQP

Every supplier to Ford, GM, and Chrysler knows that a requirement to providing parts and services is reliability. And, the reliability is assured through statistical methods, including capability analyses we are teaching now in healthcare. Achieving reliability begins with the planning phase of a new vehicle program and continues throughout the life of production. And, defects found later in the product life cycle are not discounted. Extensive warranty return analysis continues and often products and services are enhanced for reliability. The Failure Mode and Effects Analysis is a living document updated by engineering and often shared with the frontline to engage everyone in higher reliability. The process begins with communication of concept and some degree of specifications, although specifications may evolve as the capability of the technology allows reliability. A quick validation of how capability and reliability must be demonstrated first is with Toyota and the telematics technology that goes into OnStar and BMW Assist.

Motorola originally developed OnStar for Toyota. Toyota wanted to use the data that were provided via telecommunications to add value to the driver and passengers such as location services and provide a new level of safety. Most know that OnStar's and BMW's technology will automatically call for help if the air bag deploys in an accident. In the process that I am about to share, Toyota found that the capability and reliability of this emerging technology were just not sufficient yet. Toyota backed away, and Motorola found GM interested and thus pursued and have been delivering the products to GM ever since.

APQP and production part approval process (PPAP) are the methods guiding the design of the product and the process that provides the value to the ultimate customer. APQP and PPAP are used for both physical products and services and ultimately are a production process that Ford, GM, Chrysler, and Toyota, and suppliers use.

We will start with APQP. The teams should use the timing chart in Figure 11.1 to guide them in the design through launch. I will cover the timing chart and its elements and how it designs in reliability.

High reliability depends on knowing what the customers value and communicating these values in the service with measures that are specific and are correlated with expectations. In oncology, patients want to be cured, but the complexity and discomfort provide design opportunities that are far beyond just treating the cancer. Designing a cancer center nowadays includes environment and architecture that are conducive to the physical, mental, and social desires of the patient. APQP will have these values well defined and specified so that capability and reliability may be measured

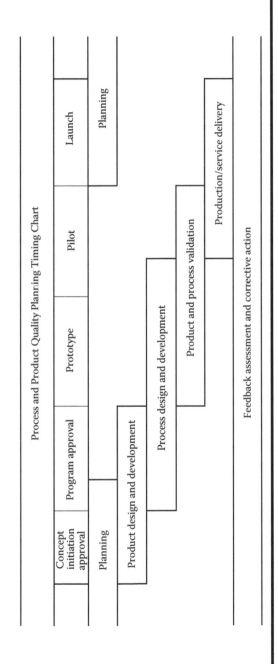

Figure 11.1 APQP timing chart. (From Automotive Industry Action Group, Ford Motor Company, General Motors, DaimlerChrysler, *AIAG Reference Manual*, 1995, Second Ed., APQP, PPAP, Capability vs. Performance from AIAG SPC reference manuals.)

and tested before accepting patients. Realizing that reliability comes from preventing defects, the team concentrates on how defects and dissatisfaction may arise and uses design failure mode and effects analysis (DFMEA) to think what defects may occur, acts by designing high yields all along the patient's journey, and ensures that controls are in place to sustain the experience. The best way to design any product or process is to simultaneously design the building and processes of care with teams working concurrently, not sequentially. Too often, designers, specifically architects, design and then hand off to the organization with little regard to the staff who work the healthcare processes and have to live with the design.

Leaders and engineers: Require a DFMEA with in-depth details of all the defect opportunities before signing off on a design.

We will discuss process and system FMEAs in the "System FMEA" section. Ensure that they are in the contract, and clear ongoing responsibilities from the design team if failures or close calls appear. Measure the design team on having a well-thought-out DFMEA, manage to this measure by using it when-ever reliability is questioned, and make it easier for the teams to use the FMEAs by posting them online for all staff to view.

Reliability is achieved through continuous improvement. The *AIAG Reference Manual* (1995) includes the plan–do–check–act (PDCA) cycle with more detail on the APQP process. See Figure 11.2.

In Figure 11.2, I share a modified graphic that was provided originally by the AIAG sharing the elements and steps of APQP. The AIAG is the central group that is supported by the automotive manufacturers, which provides the manuals for education, training, and standard work.

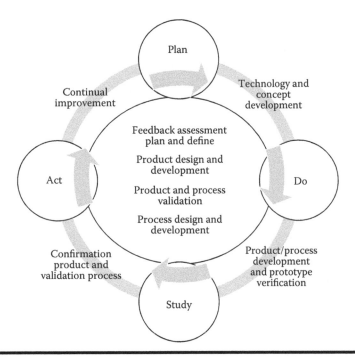

Figure 11.2   APQP example of PDCA cycle and APQP stages.

Leaders: If this diagram is familiar to you, please share how your organization uses it in healthcare on this book's website for others to see how it builds higher reliability from the beginning. Please share also how you reinforce your partners either before patients reach your organization and after discharge. Share how you require from your internal and external teams prior to launching a service whether it is a new surgical service line, a new magnetic resonance imaging (MRI), or your clinical rounding process; you should consider yourself one in a thousand in healthcare. In automotive, not doing APQP gets you fired as a supplier and supports your competition in winning another sale.

Let us dissect to learn the APQP process element by element.

On stage 1, the planning element never really begins and never ends. An HRO is continually scanning for ways to provide more value to its clients. Note the open-ended beginning and ending after the launch. This stage details and highlights the voice of the customer requirements that are critical in achieving high reliability. This stage's inputs are the following:

■ The voice of the customer including market research, prior failures, litigation, and feedback on quality from similar services
■ Business and marketing plan
■ Product and process capability studies and benchmark data
■ Assumptions listed about the product and process
■ Product reliability studies
■ Targeted and past customer inputs

The key outputs (deliverables) from the first planning stage are

■ Design goals
■ Reliability and quality goals

One can see that an HRO begins with reliability—it is not considered a given and bypassed. Reliability is detailed and considered primary to the design. This deliverable includes mean time between events or failures in similar designs and results of long-term reliability and durability tests. We continue with more outputs from the planning stage:

■ Preliminary materials and components list
■ Preliminary process flow chart
■ Preliminary listing of special needs and process characteristics

■ Product/service ensurance plan (a quality management
  system to ensure reliability)
■ Management support

Stage 2 is the product design and development. The design
takes on a near-final form, and the DFMEA is an output showing how reliability might be compromised and more importantly
how the design prevents or at least detects early signs of failure
to prevent failure at the customer, patient, and staff. The AIAG
manual shares a lesson for healthcare in its application of a system Failure Mode and Effects Analysis. This system-wide look
at how variables in a complex organization must be studied
to predict and prevent failure is exactly what helps us prevent
readmissions and complications such as surgical site infections
before during and post admission and stay. Think of population
health as a system of many input variables and a process with
outcomes that are all happening within a system where costs
are key in driving the health of the population.

The design team should consider all factors, regardless if a
factor or input is controlled. These factors may be owned or
controlled by a supplier, a provider who is not an employee
of the organization, a patient, a postdischarge facility, or any
entity that may affect the reliability of the patient's healing.
Time and again, we hear complaints about how one healthcare organization does not control another entity that is
responsible for an infection, a readmission, or other unfavorable events. In an accountable care organization, the mindset
is to acknowledge the risk and implement capability and control to prevent failure regardless of where the inputs that are
failing occur. This is like an airplane manufacturer accepting
that heavy rain may reduce the braking power on a wet run-
way and chalking it up to bad luck. Antiskid braking systems
were developed by airplane manufacturers to improve the reliability of their industry. They did not shirk the responsibility
of maintaining reliability and safety just because wet runways
are outside of the manufacturer's control.

The output is a design of product where performance and reliability can be achieved at full demand, under known circumstances, and with labor and capital resources and variation of such. Emergency rooms get busier at some times more than others. That is known, and high reliability achieves design specifications in wait times throughout the demand fluctuations. I get frustrated when telephone auto-attendant programs state, "We apologize for the longer-than-expected wait times. Rest assured that you are important to us and that we will be with you as soon as possible." Well, do you really think callers are important to them because they did not design in capability to handle volumes that they knew could occur because they went to the trouble of programming a response for when calls were not answered in a timely manner? They do not care enough to be reliable.

Inputs are the outputs of the prior stage. The outputs of stage 2 are

- DFMEA.
- Design for service or manufacturability and assembly. This is a key element for drug compounding, discharge preparation and process, and imaging.
- Design verification.
- Design review.
- Prototypes.
- Drawings and documentation of the design and process.
- Specifications from the patients and the process owners.
- Materials and supplies specifications.
- Change process for materials, supplies, and drawings.

One can refer to the *AIAG Reference Manual* (1995) for more details on each stage. I want to highlight the key outputs by stage in regard to reliability so that both leaders and engineers can appreciate that achieving high reliability is a process, is documented, and works. I invite everyone to use the manual immediately on any existing program or future. Please share your thoughts and outcomes at http://www.rpmexec.com/reliability.

Stage 3, process design and development, is to achieve reliability in the production or delivery of the product or service. Stage 2 developed the design and DFMEA. Stage 3 includes the design of the process and its process failure mode and effects analysis (PFMEA).

The outputs are as follows:

- Delivery standards examples such as discharge instruction packs in the medium that best helps the patient.
- Product/process quality system review includes a checklist for the team, which includes reliability needs such as capability studies, a training check if everyone has been trained on SPC, and an action plan that is based on the SPC results.
- Process flow chart to focus on the system, not just the individual steps in the patient's journey. This flow chart, or supplier, input, process step, output, customer (SIPOC) map, most importantly includes the inputs to each step to help the team identify the sources of variation that may hinder reliability. This map is a direct input to the next FMEA, which is described in the next item.
- PFMEA is a living document in that it is to be created before starting the service and throughout the life of the process as new learning occurs in risks and controls.
- Floor plans are key and should highlight job aids such as the Universal Protocol in every surgical area, equipment such as crash cart locations, and previous and post areas to help think system versus isolated silos of activity.
- Characteristics matrix is an analytical technique, often graphical, showing how a critical-to-quality characteristic, such as prepping the surgical site, is affected by hair removal prior to washing preparation and affects wound care after surgery.
- Prelaunch control plan.
- Process instructions and job aids.
- Measurement systems analysis plan such as lactate-level measurement methods, timing, and interpretation.

- Preliminary process capability study plan, which is key to reliability. When healthcare routinely reports on capability, we will be able to truly assess reliability. Again, reliability is not about standard work; it is about capability to meet requirements and be sustained for the intended time.
- Packaging and follow-up with patients for continued healing.
- Management support is especially noted as an output of process design because too often, designers run rough-shod over process designers, and this affects the reliability and satisfaction of the people in the processes. Ultimately, the patients experience undesirable outcomes and less favorable experiences.

Stage 4, product and process validation, is all about testing the capability in meeting the design and customer requirements while *warming up the process* prior to full launch with patients.
The outputs are the following:

- Production trial run statistics measured using capability studies with SPC on key characteristics.
- Measurement systems evaluation, which can include if the laboratory results are accurate when starting a new laboratory. Another example is something as simple as a bed management system truthfully showing the status of patient room readiness. Healthcare is notoriously struggling with bed visibility that $39-a-night motels have had for years. In London, we actually found a free bed management system on the Internet. It is a travesty that the struggles and costs that healthcare runs into in trying to acquire a good measurement system of such a critical characteristic—the bed availability of an emergency department patient.
- Preliminary process capability study. The plan was completed in the prior stage. Now, it is time to use a statistical capability study during the pilot. Findings must end with improvements.

- Production part approval by the engineers and the patients who represent the future patients of this design. AIAG has a well-developed process for this element. It is titled production part approval process and is as important and required by automotive, aviation, aerospace, and electrical safety products and services as this APQP process.
- Production validation testing ensures that there are clear requirements needing validation, and the pilot gives us capability of the testing performance. At present, there is much debate about the efficacy of prostate cancer testing and further debate about the need.
- Packaging/instruction evaluation again validates that critical information such as discharge instructions are sufficient, understandable, and easily available to the staff so that it is easier to ensure that patients receive the information.
- Production control plan, which includes control plans that are readily available and being used, as well as staff instructions, and measurement systems in place.
- Quality planning sign-off and management support confirm that this APQP process is being followed and effective.

Stage 5 is for feedback, assessment, and corrective action and is ongoing for continuous improvement.

Its outputs are

- Capability
- Reliability
- Reduce variation
- Elimination of escaping defects
- Postdischarge quality

We need to take many of the same statistical methods and apply them with the front line in designing and running our healthcare processes.

FMEA Case Studies

Cedars-Sinai was in the news years ago for overradiating 200 patients in imaging. I was working with Cedars-Sinai on other quality improvements and asked them if the imaging equipment manufacturer had supplied their FMEA showing that they had thought through the natural inclination to adjust controls on the equipment to get a higher-quality image. The person at Cedars-Sinai went to investigate the FMEA. What is your guess if she received an FMEA?

An acute care hospital in a well-to-do area of Northern California had a computerized tomography (CT) fail. It took days before it was in operation again. Can you imagine the extra anxiety of patients waiting days for a CT scan? Worse, there was a patient waiting on a CT who had been told by a hospitalist before the scan that the cancer had spread and that it could be terminal. The oncology physician calmed the patient and put the delay into perspective that it would have no effect on treatment or would not create additional risks.

Yet, a son had flown across the country to be with the patient and surely had expected to be taking his parent home days before. There was no backup other than a positron emission tomography (PET) scan. We found out about the CT going down from this patient and his son. We spoke with the oncologist and investigated with the vice-president (VP) of the imaging department who immediately got involved with his team on when the CT scanner would be back in operation to expedite this patient's needs.

An HRO works with its suppliers who are a critical component of achieving reliability.

I suggested to the VP that he ask the supplier for its FMEA and find specifically the failure mode occurring with the CT. In automotive and aerospace, we expected our customer to ask for the FMEA. We would have already had a team working on the FMEA and control prior to the customer calling if we found the failure or soon after if the customer found the failure. In any failure, we knew that there was a weakness in the process, and the FMEA did not fully identify a new variable or a weakness in the control plan. If this failure mode was completely missing on the FMEA, we had more work to do, and an increased state of mindfulness occurred because we *missed it*.

> An FMEA is to first "think" how a process may fail, "act" before it fails or at least fail-safe so that nothing escapes to the customer, and then "control" the process to prevent failures from reaching the customer.

We never saw the imaging equipment supplier's FMEA as of this writing. Healthcare has a long way to go to achieve high reliability, and making the FMEA a standard deliverable prior to receiving the first product or service from a supplier will do wonders in higher reliability. And, above all, do not be embarrassed to ask for the FMEA. Many of the companies supplying products and services to healthcare have units that supply industries that demand FMEAs and other concepts in this book including the most important concept—capability analyses.

The FMEA is not complex or difficult to learn. Yes, it can be tedious. Yes, every service line, every department, and every piece of capital equipment should have an FMEA. Yes, it will take years for healthcare to get to where automotive and electrical safety industries are, but the culture change associated with performing FMEAs before launch will accelerate healthcare's journey to higher reliability.

> The FMEA is intended to be, and must be, a living document.

This means that we need to keep it handy in the design and the workplace so that people continue to learn how a process might fail and then how to act to prevent failure. Think that if the FMEA was posted in the CT area and the team could have quickly found the failure mode and had a control plan how to recover? Sure, it might have said to contact the supplier, but then the team could work with the supplier and the FMEA to find the weakness in the FMEA and perhaps discover the variation that occurred resulting in the FMEA to prevent the next one.

Posting the FMEA is not new thinking. While touring a Ford engine plant, I saw an excerpt from an FMEA and a picture of a failed engine right on the equipment making the engine and in full view of any person operating the machine. The picture of the failure brought the voice of the customers and the voice of the process designers, the FMEA, to everyone's attention.

Engineers: Learn about the FMEA for design, process, and system.

Try the FMEA using the form on my website, and tell me how it worked for you and your team. Do not get bogged down on the ratings. Understand that they are relative within the process or product that you are working on. Take the highest risk that you think you have; use higher values in the severity, occurrence, and detection ratings for that risk, and this calibrates your team's judgment throughout the FMEA. Do not get bogged down arguing about a difference of one, two, or three points because it is subjective anyway. The purpose of the FMEA is to prioritize where higher reliability is needed. Take the top few risks, and get controls in the process to prevent failure. Move on to the next risks by engaging the people who design and do the work. Use the FMEA to collaborate with users, such as imaging and robotic technicians and surgeons. They will better understand how they can increase the risks and can learn from the FMEA what actions are risky.

System FMEA

A system FMEA is an all-encompassing FMEA of design and process FMEAs. The overradiation of 200 patients could have been prevented by a system FMEA outlook of the risks. The manufacturer of the imaging equipment should have both a design and a process FMEA. The manufacturer should also have an FMEA covering their imaging equipment in the healthcare organization's environment. This FMEA would include the variables of technicians' and radiologists' natural desire to get the best image possible and thus find a way to increase the radiation, which is a major variable when it comes to image quality. The manufacturer or user would lead the system FMEA with these parties who are involved and ideally in the actual environment where the imaging equipment will be operated.

I understand that healthcare has a long way to go to get even the design and process FMEAs in place. As these FMEAs are created, think of the environment where the system will be used, and use the design and process FMEAs as surrogates for now. If a failure occurs and is not found in the design or process FMEA, it might be because of interactions in the system that were missed and not entirely a design or process failure. So, simply add it to the process FMEA and keep it living.

Healthcare Clinical Standards and CoPs in Reliability Design

When we think of TJC and CMS, many know that they developed and created many of the standards throughout the world. And, they continue to educate healthcare on those standards and continually improve them. TJC actually originated many of today's standards that were used by CMS when it was created in the 1960s. CMS now calls these standards *conditions of participation* as they focus on accrediting organizations that care for Medicare and Medicaid patients.

Healthcare organizations earn the right to participate in these programs. Unfortunately, even these standards hinder healthcare's appreciation for reliability. The standards and CoPs are essentially minimal levels of performance to participate in reimbursement programs or to maintain a minimal level of accreditation. The standards are not the benchmarks of excellence. To work just to standards is to work to be average or even less than average.

To remove the standards without the methods and discipline of high reliability would most likely lower healthcare reliability overall because the reinforcements for high reliability are not yet in healthcare. Just as recently as 2012, CMS started reducing reimbursement for low reliability. We will cover this further in Chapter 15, but keep in mind throughout this book that there are healthcare organizations today that can continue to do business regardless of major harm and poor reliability. Their days are hopefully numbered as healthcare begins to use the high-reliability methods in this book.

Leaders: Invite conversation among your clinicians on CoPs that they are repeatedly going beyond the minimal level.

Discover why, and one will most likely hear that their quality of care is too important to them and their patients to just do the standard. Thank them for this high-reliability mindset. Then, engage them in taking standards that they struggle to meet and improve them. Report back and look for these new levels of reliability in the FMEA's control plan including measurement to better manage to the measure.

Today, one may never hear the term capability or reliability in walks around the healthcare organization. Those days are soon to be numbered, I think. Just last week, I heard the head of risk management respond to a close call saying, "This is not high reliability."

High reliability is taking way too long from my vantage point as I work in the hospitals, ambulatory centers, clinics, and countless other healthcare sites. This is why I write. We have to find faster ways to spread the benefits to patients, staff, and healthcare cost. We have to find ways to spread the methods that HROs achieve high reliability. And, it is best done by those who have lived it because there are so many ways to fail in complex industries like healthcare, and identifying those risks in advance from experience will speed healthcare in its journey.

Healthcare executives and staff tend to have careers only in healthcare. So, we cannot expect them to have these experiences—yet. In automotive and electrical safety, we had oligopolies, which cared enough about reliability to share how to achieve it with their staff and suppliers. They took it on themselves to educate, train, and reinforce high reliability.

Healthcare is a very fragmented industry, and customers nowadays have little power over a hospital. The balance of power is shifting though as major employers start negotiating directly with the healthcare organizations on behalf of not only themselves but also the individual employees. Walmart, Intel, and Caterpillar are just a few of these major employers that are demanding higher reliability for their populations and lower cost.

A healthcare organization that achieves higher reliability should stand out with major employers which are HROs, such as Caterpillar, Eaton, and SKF. A healthcare HRO should have an advantage in both quality and cost.

Chapter 12

Rolled Throughput Yield

Introduction

In Chapters 1 through 11, we learned about capability, and now we will learn how Deming's theories used in high-reliability organizations (HROs) help us understand health-care's complexity better. Deming's coaching to take a systems approach is explained using his Theory of Escaping Defects and a concept named *rolled throughput yield (RTY)*, which has been taught in reliability classes and Six Sigma for years. We will relate these concepts to those of value streams, a term that is commonly used by some healthcare organizations.

Theories of Escaping Defects and RTY

Deming's Theory of Escaping Defects supports the finding of rolled throughput yield. RTY is measured using the following variables:

- Yield = area under the probability density curve between tolerances.
- First-time yield = nondefective *units* from a process.

Note: First time yield does not offer a chance to estimate the probability of a defect opportunity that may "escape to the customer."

■ Throughput yield (first time through yield) = nondefective *opportunities* from a process step.
  – Defect opportunities = number of potential defects within one product or service. One product may have multiple defects and thus increase the probability of defectives.
■ RTY provides a chance to estimate the probability of creating a defect opportunity = product of each process step's yield in units (1 – defects per unit [DPU])
■ RTY = (throughput yield$_1$ × throughput yield$_2$ × throughput yield$_3$…throughput yield$_n$)
  where throughput yield = DPU = number of defects per unit.

So, simply multiply the throughput yields that were calculated for each process step.

Figure 12.1 takes us step by step in calculating yield statistics, which helps us understand Deming's concepts of RTY and his Theory of Escaping Defects. The statistics are DPU and defects-per-million opportunities (DPMO), which are commonly used in conjunction with sigma level. These variables and their calculations are detailed step by step in Figure 12.1.

RTY Defined

W. Edwards Deming and every good performance improvement training program teach how the yield at the end of the process is affected by the yield at each step along the way. As a patient moves through the healthcare process, his or her probability of achieving a perfect quality outcome is a function of the quality at every step along his or her journey.

Using surgery as an example, we found that the patients undergoing one of the most common procedures, total knee

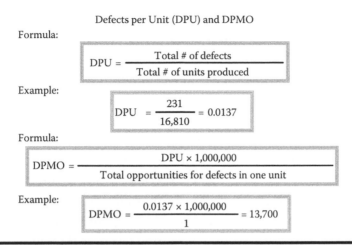

Figure 12.1 Defects per unit (DPU) and defects-per-million opportunities (DPMO) calculated.

replacement (TKR), have fewer complications and lower readmissions when quality is achieved from their first visit with the surgeon through days after discharge. See a simplified view of the surgical patient's journey in Figure 12.2.

Some surgeons have very low readmission rates. We found that they have a high-quality sense of potential complications based on the individual patient's risk factors. These surgeons will tailor a preparation plan for patients even to the point of delaying or not doing surgery until the risk factors are managed. Their quality, or yield in terms of not letting a patient enter surgery until ready, is high. In surgery,

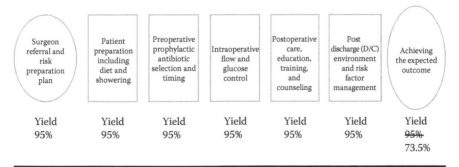

Figure 12.2 Rolled throughput yield (RTY) for a total knee replacement (TKR).

research has shown that the length of the procedure and blood glucose control can lead to a better outcome with fewer complications.

Surgeons, anesthesiologists, and surgical staff who perform well as a team may be considered having a higher yield intra-operatively compared to those teams that have longer procedure times and do not manage glucose levels as well. Now, in recovery postoperative, inpatient stay, and post discharge, quality again is key. The blood glucose control, physical therapy, nutrition, case management, home preparation to reduce the fall risks, and counselling all can vary in quality and affect the outcomes and risk for surgical site infections or damage to the knee.

The probability of the expected outcome for a patient is not the average yield along the journey. The probability, or yield, as the patient *rolls through* the TKR process is much less at approximately only 73.5%. In other words, over 25% of the patients experience worse than they could have despite having a process where each step's quality is 95%.

The lesson Deming taught about RTY is that quality must be achieved every step of the way, not just at the end. To achieve quality at the end of a process, we need to achieve capability and control at every step.

Inspection Is Not Reliable

And, inspection to sort out bad things at the end of the process is not reliable if we think that we can get by not improving every step in a process. I teach the classic "Letter F story." See Figure 12.3. In this simple exercise, the class inspects for the letter F in a story resulting in a count of the number of Fs found. Seldom does anyone get the count correct thus proving that inspection is not very reliable in sorting out the good from the bad. Try it with your

The necessity of training farmhands for the first-class farms in the fatherly handling of farm livestock is foremost in the eyes of the farm owners. Since the forefathers of the farm owners trained the farmhands for first class farms in the fatherly handling of farm livestock, the farm owners felt they should carry on with the family tradition of training farm hands of the first class farmers in the fatherly handling of farm livestock because they believe that it is the basis of good fundamental farm management.

Figure 12.3   Inspecting exercise by counting a letter's occurrence.

teammates, and, better yet, in a small group. Ask each member to count the letter Fs, upper case or lower case does not matter, and record the count. The correct count of Fs is 22.

Using a histogram like in Figure 12.4 for even more fun with statistics, plot the frequency of each total that is counted. It goes something like this. See, your group just proved that we better have very high yields all along the way the first time because relying on inspection to sort out poor yields is not very reliable. It depends on if you are counting defective units (sentences) or defects within the unit (misspellings, punctuation, grammar, etc.).

The voice of the customer is often about defective units, whereas to achieve the highest quality, measure all defects to prevent defective units.

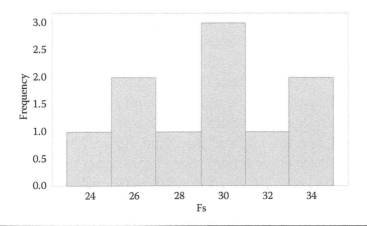

Figure 12.4   The frequency of the letter Fs counted.

Total Knee and Hip Replacement and Reliability

Healthcare is complex. The TKR example in Figure 12.2 for RTY is vastly simplified. A more detailed map of the patient's journey undergoing elective TKRs is shown in Figure 12.5.

Imagine the yields across these steps and the RTY that is possible after so many steps. Procedures like TKR require every step to be highly reliable to ensure a reliable outcome. The rate of readmissions for an elective TKR varies from 2% to beyond 16% and can go higher with specific populations of patients with high-risk factors. We have to consider the quality at every step beginning with the first visit to a surgeon through months after the procedure.

The Centers for Medicare & Medicaid (CMS), in fact, are now penalizing acute care hospitals up to 3% of their total annual reimbursement for excess readmissions in CMS' value-based purchasing program to reinforce quality over fee for service. Fee for service is a major factor in healthcare not becoming a highly reliable organization. Fee for service is how healthcare has been paid for years, and it is now shifting to how HROs get reimbursed—value. In fee for service, healthcare organizations get paid for whatever services they provide regardless of quality.

Unbelievably, hospitals used to get paid twice when they did not have quality care and a patient was readmitted, even if the hospital caused the reason for readmission. An example of dysfunctional reinforcement is when a patient who gets an infection while in the hospital has to return to be treated, and the hospital gets paid again. What is worse is when a hospital gets paid more for holding the patient longer, and every minute longer raises the risk of getting an infection. Those days are slowly going away. I can tell you that General Motors (GM) or Ford would not pay for defective products, and it was our responsibility to bring the defective product back at our expense.

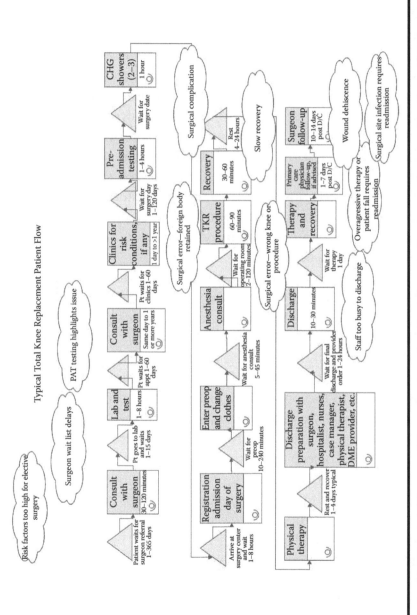

Figure 12.5   Elective total knee or hip replacement patient flow and common factors affecting reliable outcomes. CHG, chlorhexidine gluconate; DME, durable medical equipment; PAT, preadmission testing.

Figure 12.5 is a more realistic flow of steps that the patients go through in a typical elective TKR. In addition to thinking of the yields across all these steps and the resulting diminishing probability of a perfect outcome, consider the factors in the captions along the patient's journey.

At one hospital, New Hanover Regional Medical Center (NHRMC), a team of surgeons, hospitalists, physician assistants, nurse practitioners, nurses, therapists, administrators, and ancillary staff identified more than 10 factors with their patients, their processes, and processes outside of their hospitals that statistically correlated with their patients coming back within 30 days of discharge. Just reading the last sentence should give one an appreciation of the many steps and multiple geographical sites that can contribute to a readmission, and do not forget the patient's unique risk factors such as anemia and other health factors.

Even this map is simplified compared to reality, and it shows common quality and productivity issues. While we focus on clinical outcomes here, note the wastes of time, which can go on for years when patients do not achieve risk-reduction plans such as lowering their body mass index or quitting smoking. Both of these factors can contribute percentage points to the probability of readmission. I am covering only elective TKR versus trauma cases in this story, and surgeons do not have to operate on these patients. Therefore, it can take years before the patients would have lowered their risks well enough for a safe surgery and rehabilitation.

Although in our infancy in the United States, transparency of complications, quality, and readmissions by surgeon and surgical center are visible through patients. My brother, Mark, recently went through a hip procedure, and he had done his homework in choosing the best surgeon and site for his procedure. Everything went well for him, as it does for 95% of patients, but I credit our mother for keeping him safe as she stayed with him during his recovery. Not everyone has his or her mother to keep him or her safe.

Someday, healthcare will have transparent clinical outcomes that really matter to patients such as statistics on knee and hip functionality over time. The current so-called clinical outcome metrics are really safety metrics.

Defects and Abnormalities

High reliability depends on reducing or eliminating defects along the process as we saw in the concept of RTY. Understanding what one means by a defect is key. One person may be counting defective events, such as the number of wrong-site surgeries that are performed, while another person may be counting the number of defects in the surgery process that led to the wrong-site surgery event. The former example is one of defective units, and the latter is when we are measuring the DPU.

The customers, or the patients, usually measure defective events. A highly reliable organization measures defective events, but it lowers them by reducing the DPU. It is kind of like the Y and the x equation again. To get a lower count of surgeries that result in harm, we reduce the number of defects, such as confusing consent forms, missing patient IDs, and pauses before surgical entry that are not thoughtfully and seriously performed.

I cover several terms that are similar to the term *defect* because healthcare uses a variety of terms relating to things that go wrong. I think that we all know that variation is a defect when not desired, such as in prepping skin before surgery or not, using clippers instead of razors to remove hair from the surgical site if needed, and in the timing of antibiotic before surgical entry. Variation outside of healthcare may be exactly what we pay for such as in jazz improvisation. But, let us consider variation in this book to be undesired.

Behavioral slips, lapses, and mistakes are terms that are used to describe defects. James Reason teaches us about abnormalities. HROs work to reduce all the defects to improve outcomes and improve safety specifically. Examples of behavioral slips include rushing instruction to a patient because we are in a hurry. A lapse can be completely forgetting to provide instruction to the patient. A mistake can be giving the wrong instruction to the patient. We have confused patients with all the instructions for recovering from a TKR.

For one organization, several surgeons had their own discharge instructions in addition to the hospital's discharge instructions. The nurse skimmed over most of the written instructions and highlighted a couple of them such as the need to inspect the wound for signs of infection. Skipped was the need to control diet and how to replace the bandage to reduce the risk of infection. We could call this an example of any of the three terms. A slip may be accurate if the nurse did not cover vital details because of many details. A lapse could define the error in that there may not have been enough time to prepare the patient. A mistake could be judged if not managing time well enough to cover the instructions.

Regardless, HROs work to prevent all the defects, and they start by measuring all of them; managing to the slips, lapses, and mistakes in real time; and making it easier for the providers and staff to help patients be capable of care after discharge.

Theory of Escaping Defects

Now that we understand RTY and defects, we can appreciate and act using Deming's *Theory of Escaping Defects*. This theory has been the foundational concept in our work on improving reliability. We have used this theory in eliminating wrong-site surgeries, mortality from sepsis, surgical site infections, and preventing failure in achieving zero defects exceeding five years.

We know that the way to eliminate failures is to reduce the defects. In context now as we explain the Theory of Escaping Defects, a failure is an outcome such as a surgeon operating on the wrong knee. When I have investigated wrong-site surgeries, invariably there were smaller failures, defects that occurred leading up to the final failure, cutting on the wrong knee. Often, we found defects in the consent form, such as someone wrote the wrong laterality on the form, or the laterality was not stated. Writing on the wrong laterality is a defect that contributed to the failure.

Usually, we find more than one defect, and the other common defect is the absence of the attending surgeon during the *time out*. The time out should occur immediately before the surgeon puts the knife to skin. In one hospital, it was the norm for the surgical team to do the time out before the surgeon is scrubbed and in the operating room. This is an example of *pencil whipping* at its worst, a term that clinicians use when people input that a task was done when in fact it was not. A time out is to be done by the entire surgical team and especially with the person performing the procedure. After all, how many wrong-site surgeries have occurred due to the scrub technician making the incision on the wrong patient or body part?

Checklists in Healthcare—Self-Inspection

One article reports that the World Health Organization (WHO) Surgical Safety Checklist has not resulted in a reduction in failures, specifically mortality. We can use this discussion to explore reliability in a measurement system. In the article published in the *New England Journal of Medicine*, "Introduction of Surgical Safety Checklists in Ontario, Canada,"[1] the authors found no statistically significant reduction in mortality or complications. Conversely, the WHO reports significant reductions in mortality. Let us examine the study that was done in Canada first.

The rate of any complication at all sites dropped from 11.0% at baseline to 7.0% after introduction of the checklist ($P < 0.001$); the total in-hospital rate of death dropped from 1.5% to 0.8% ($P = 0.003$) (Figure 12.6).[2]

The overall rates of surgical site infection and unplanned reoperation also declined significantly ($P < 0.001$ and $P = 0.047$, respectively). This was a population-based study of surgical safety checklists in Ontario hospitals upon the first introduction of the WHO checklist. The study reports no significant reduction in operative mortality (71% before and 0.65% after checklist introduction), nor did the checklist result in reductions in the risks of surgical complications, emergency department visits, or hospital readmissions within 30 days after discharge.

I have witnessed hundreds of surgical teams using, or reported to be using, the WHO Surgical Safety Checklist from London, England to California. There is tremendous variation in the use of the checklist both in the checklist itself and the sincerity of the checking. A checklist should be an aid, not a hindrance, for those who were using it. The leaders of HROs know that anything too cumbersome without perceived benefit and without being reinforced by leadership will not achieve its intended effect and, in fact, may compromise reliability and safety.

Safety devices on power tools are often so cumbersome; users bypass the safety all together making the tool less safe than if the safety device was never installed. I have a battery-powered circular saw that I never use because I can barely operate it while holding the safety. If I had to use it frequently, I am certain that I would bypass the safety device. I wonder what the company was thinking. I imagine someone who is more interested in preventing liability claims rather than someone who had to use the saw that is designed with the safety device.

Table 5. Outcomes before and after Checklist Implementation, According to Site.*

Site No.	No. of Patients Enrolled		Surgical-Site Infection		Unplanned Return to the Operating Room		Pneumonia		Death		Any Complication	
	Before	After	Before	After	Before	After	Before	After	Before	After	Before	After
							percent					
1	524	598	4.0	2.0	4.6	1.8	0.8	1.2	1.0	0.0	11.6	7.0
2	357	351	2.0	1.7	0.6	1.1	3.6	3.7	1.1	0.3	7.8	6.3
3	497	486	5.8	4.3	4.6	2.7	1.6	1.7	0.8	1.4	13.5	9.7
4	520	545	3.1	2.6	2.5	2.2	0.6	0.9	1.0	0.6	7.5	5.5
5	370	330	20.5	3.6	1.4	1.8	0.3	0.0	1.4	0.0	21.4	5.5
6	496	476	4.0	4.0	3.0	3.2	2.0	1.9	3.6	1.7	10.1	9.7
7	525	585	9.5	5.8	1.3	0.2	1.0	1.7	2.1	1.7	12.4	8.0
8	444	584	4.1	2.4	0.5	1.2	0.0	0.0	1.4	0.3	6.1	3.6
Total	3733	3955	6.2	3.4	2.4	1.8	1.1	1.3	1.5	0.8	11.0	7.0
P value			<0.001		0.047		0.46		0.003		<0.001	

* The most common complications occurring during the first 30 days of hospitalization after the operation are listed. Bold type indicates values that were significantly different (at P<0.05) before and after checklist implementation, on the basis of P values calculated by means of the chi-square test or Fisher's exact test. P values are shown for the comparison of the total value after checklist implementation as compared with the total value before implementation.

Figure 12.6   Rate of complications. (From http://www.nejm.org/doi/full/10.1056/NEJMsa1308261.)

In designing checklists, Boeing understands very well that a checklist that takes too long to properly use is worthless. Boeing's article, "Flight Crew Response to In-Flight Smoke, Fire, or Fumes," describes some of the design characteristics in making checklists.[3]

The checklist shown in Figure 12.7 is one that could be modified for surgical fires. Surgical fires occur more than 550 times a year in the United States according to Emergency Care Research Institute (ECRI).[4] In the Food and Drug Administration (FDA) website, the FDA adds that surgical fires are preventable.[5]

Airlines have long provided flight crews with checklists to help them identify and deal with smoke, fire, and fumes. See Figure 12.7.

Until recently, manufacturer and airline checklists varied in format and content. In response to this situation, Boeing worked together with airlines, pilots, and other manufacturers to develop a philosophy and a checklist template to standardize and optimize flight crew responses to nonalerted smoke, fire, or fume (SFF) events (i.e., events not annunciated to the flight crew by onboard detection systems).

The checklist design incorporates a common approach for manufacturers and airlines to take when developing checklists. The checklist includes actions for pilots to execute across multiple models.

Many readers may have heard of cockpit resource management (CRM) aka crew resource management. CRM was taken to heart at United Airlines (UAL) after the investigation of UAL's last fatal crash caused by human error found that the culture in the cockpit was hindering communication and action. The navigator's repeated warnings of low fuel were ignored by the captain, which resulted in the crash. Interestingly, the first task in using the checklist for SFF reads, "The entire crew must be part of the solution." This is the story of Flight 173.

STEP	ACTION	RESPONSE
1	Diversion may be required.	
2	Oxygen masks (if required)	On, 100%
3	Smoke goggles (if required)	On
4	Crew and cabin communications	Establish
5	Manufacturer's initial steps	Accomplish
	Anytime smoke or fumes become the greatest threat, accomplish separate *Smoke or Fumes Removal Checklist*.	
6	Source is immediately obvious and can be extinguished quickly: If YES go to Step 7. If NO go to Step 9.	
7	Extinguish the source. If possible, remove power from affected equipment by switch or circuit breaker on the flight deck or in the cabin.	
8	Source is visually confirmed to be extinguished: If YES consider reversing manufacturer's initial steps. Go to Step 17. If NO go to Step 9.	
9	Remaining minimal essential manufacturer's action steps [These are steps that do not meet the "initial steps" criteria but are probable sources.]	Accomplish
10	Initiate a diversion to the nearest suitable airport while continuing the checklist.	
	Warning: If the smoke/fire/fumes situation becomes unmanageable, consider an immediate landing.	
11	Landing is imminent: If YES go to Step 16. If NO go to Step 12.	
12	"X" system actions [These are further actions to control/extinguish source.] If dissipating, go to Step 16.	Accomplish
13	"Y" system actions [These are further actions to control/extinguish source.] If dissipating, go to Step 16.	Accomplish
14	"Z" system actions [These are further actions to control/extinguish source.] If dissipating, go to Step 16.	Accomplish
15	SFF continues after all system-related steps are accomplished: Consider landing immediately. Go to Step 16.	
16	Review Operational Considerations.	
17	Accomplish *Smoke or Fumes Removal Checklist*, if required.	
18	Checklist complete.	

Figure 12.7 Checklist for responding to smoke or fire. (From McKenzie, W. A., Flight Crew Response to In-Flight Smoke, Fire, or Fumes, available at http://www.boeing.com/commercial/aeromagazine/articles/qtr_01 _09/pdfs/AERO_Q109.pdf.)

On December 28, 1978, United Airlines, Inc., Flight 173 crashed into a wooded, populated area of suburban Portland, OR, during an approach to the Portland International Airport. The aircraft had delayed southeast of the airport at a low altitude for about 1 hour,

while the flight crew coped with a landing gear malfunction and prepared the passengers for a possible
emergency landing. The aircraft was destroyed; there
was no fire. Of the 181 passengers and 8 crewmembers aboard, 8 passengers, the flight engineer, and a
flight attendant were killed, and 21 passengers and
2 crewmembers were injured seriously.

The National Transportation Safety Board determined that the probable cause of the accident was
the failure of the captain to monitor properly the
aircraft's fuel state and to properly respond to the
low fuel state and the crewmember's advisories
regarding the fuel state. This resulted in fuel exhaus-
tion to all engines. His inattention resulted from
preoccupation with a landing gear malfunction and
preparations for a possible landing emergency.

Contributing to the accident was the failure of the
other two flight crewmembers either to fully compre-
hend the criticality of the fuel state or to successfully
communicate their concern to the captain.[6]

In the WHO surgical safety checklist shown in Figure 12.8,
we actually see three checklists corresponding to the major
process steps for a surgery.

The WHO suggests tailoring the checklist for local needs.
Those not trained in designing checklists might benefit from
this article. I have seen teams expressing frustration at the
length of the WHO surgical safety checklist. Organizations
adding checks for actions that should have been checked
before admission to the surgical center have added 20 seconds
or more to the team using the checklist. The key is to have
the staff performing the work inspect their own work in the
process—not afterwards. True, until the process is reliable,
additional checks are required but more for root cause analysis
in real time and continuous improvement rather than relying
on inspection to ensure quality.

Surgical Safety Checklist (First Edition)
World Health Organization

Before induction of anaesthesia ▶▶▶▶▶▶▶▶   Before skin incision ▶▶▶▶▶▶▶▶▶▶▶   Before patient leaves operating room

SIGN IN

☐ PATIENT HAS CONFIRMED
  • IDENTITY
  • SITE
  • PROCEDURE
  • CONSENT

☐ SITE MARKED/NOT APPLICABLE

☐ ANAESTHESIA SAFETY CHECK COMPLETED

☐ PULSE OXIMETER ON PATIENT AND FUNCTIONING

DOES PATIENT HAVE A:

KNOWN ALLERGY?
☐ NO
☐ YES

DIFFICULT AIRWAY/ASPIRATION RISK?
☐ NO
☐ YES, AND EQUIPMENT/ASSISTANCE AVAILABLE

RISK OF >500ML BLOOD LOSS
(7ML/KG IN CHILDREN)?
☐ NO
☐ YES, AND ADEQUATE INTRAVENOUS ACCESS
  AND FLUIDS PLANNED

TIME OUT

☐ CONFIRM ALL TEAM MEMBERS HAVE
  INTRODUCED THEMSELVES BY NAME AND
  ROLE

☐ SURGEON, ANAESTHESIA PROFESSIONAL
  AND NURSE VERBALLY CONFIRM
  • PATIENT
  • SITE
  • PROCEDURE

ANTICIPATED CRITICAL EVENTS

☐ SURGEON REVIEWS: WHAT ARE THE
  CRITICAL OR UNEXPECTED STEPS,
  OPERATIVE DURATION, ANTICIPATED
  BLOOD LOSS?

☐ ANAESTHESIA TEAM REVIEWS: ARE THERE
  ANY PATIENT-SPECIFIC CONCERNS?

☐ NURSING TEAM REVIEWS: HAS STERILITY
  (INCLUDING INDICATOR RESULTS) BEEN
  CONFIRMED? ARE THERE EQUIPMENT
  ISSUES OR ANY CONCERNS?

HAS ANTIBIOTIC PROPHYLAXIS BEEN GIVEN
WITHIN THE LAST 60 MINUTES?
☐ YES
☐ NOT APPLICABLE

IS ESSENTIAL IMAGING DISPLAYED?
☐ YES
☐ NOT APPLICABLE

SIGN OUT

NURSE VERBALLY CONFIRMS WITH THE
TEAM:

☐ THE NAME OF THE PROCEDURE RECORDED

☐ THAT INSTRUMENT, SPONGE AND NEEDLE
  COUNTS ARE CORRECT (OR NOT
  APPLICABLE)

☐ HOW THE SPECIMEN IS LABELLED
  (INCLUDING PATIENT NAME)

☐ WHETHER THERE ARE ANY EQUIPMENT
  PROBLEMS TO BE ADDRESSED

☐ SURGEON, ANAESTHESIA PROFESSIONAL
  AND NURSE REVIEW THE KEY CONCERNS
  FOR RECOVERY AND MANAGEMENT
  OF THIS PATIENT

THIS CHECKLIST IS NOT INTENDED TO BE COMPREHENSIVE. ADDITIONS AND MODIFICATIONS TO FIT LOCAL PRACTICE ARE ENCOURAGED.

Figure 12.8   The WHO surgical safety checklist. (From World Health Organization, entered into force in July 1948. (From the World Alliance for Patient Safety, The Surgical Safety Checklist, 2008.)

An interesting letter to the editor from an anesthesiologist in Canada reinforces Deming's Theory of Escaping Defects. My experience in watching hundreds of surgeries is similar. And, our chart of close calls was included in the early chapters from with 'My experience supports this anesthesiologist's suggestion to report near misses. Routinely, I create a daily chart of both close calls and actual events and post it daily for staff and surgeons to see their progress in eliminating these defects that will eventually result in a more serious event.

As described by Urbach et al. in the *New England Journal of Medicine* article (March 13 issue), (1) the surgical safety checklist is a tool that is designed to ensure that the incidence of errors related to communication in the operating theater is minimized.[7] (2) As Lucian Leape, MD, and Professor at Harvard School of Public Health emphasizes in the editorial accompanying the article, the diligence with which the checklist is developed and applied is critical to its effectiveness. As a cardiac anesthesiologist, I have witnessed discussions that have averted potential errors during and after surgery.

Accreditation Canada has adopted the surgical safety checklist as a required organizational practice. As an accreditor, I have evaluated approximately 10 operating rooms since the mandatory introduction of the checklist in Ontario. During these visits, I have observed that practices ranging from a thorough evaluation to a perfunctory lip-service discussion, as Leape suggests, are possible.

In order to unlock the full value of the checklist, it will be necessary to educate surgical teams on the concept of near misses. Near misses are poorly understood by healthcare professionals. When near misses are reported and analyzed, it often uncovers system deficiencies that when corrected lead to safer patient care. Thomas Diller, MD, is an expert on healthcare root cause investigation. He and his coauthors have built on James Reason's algorithm for determining just cause. Achieving reliability is very dependent on learning all that can be learned from accidents and close calls. Oversimplifying root cause investigation is an issue, according to Reason. Diller and others believe that four issues support Reason's point: (a) The use of root cause analysis is neither standardized nor reliable between organizations, (b) hospitals focus on "who" did "what" rather than on "why" the error occurred, (c) the identified causes are often too nonspecific to develop actionable correction plans, and (d) a standardized nomenclature does not exist to allow analysis of recurring errors across the organization. The authors have modified the Human Factors Analysis Classification System (HFACS), based on James Reason's theory of error causation for use in healthcare. We are using HFACS in CHRISTUS health system today and learning more that we did without this HFACS practice.[8]

Leaders and engineers: Relate RTY, defect terms, and how important it is to reduce defects at every step because of the Theory of Escaping Defects to the entire organization.

Give examples from your events and experiences. Reward people who want to start improvement teams on their processes to identify and eliminate defects. Measure the reduction in defects and reward. Reinforce those who fail to appreciate the behaviors of HROs in reducing defects continuously.

References

1. Urbach, D. R., Govindarajan, A., Saskin, R., Wilton, A. S., and Baxter, N. N. 2014. Introduction of surgical safety checklist in Ontario, Canada. *New England Journal of Medicine* 370:1029–1038.
2. Available at http://www.nejm.org/doi/full/10.1056/NEJMsa1308261.
3. McKenzie, W. A. Flight crew response to in-flight smoke, fire, or fumes. Available at http://www.boeing.com/commercial/aeromagazine/articles/qtr_01_09/pdfs/AERO_Q109.pdf.

4. ECRI Institute. 2009. New clinical guide to surgical fire prevention. *Health Devices* 38(10):314–332.

5. Preventing Surgical Fires: FDA Safety Communication. Oct. 13, 2011. Available at http://www.fda.gov/Drugs/DrugSafety /SafeUseInitiative/PreventingSurgicalFires/ucm270633.htm.

6. National Transportation Board Aircraft Accident Report. United Airlines, Inc. McDonnell-Douglas, DC-8-61, N8082U Portland, Oregon. December 28, 1978. http://www.ntsb.gov/investigations /AccidentReports/Reports/AAR7907.pdf.

7. World Health Organization, entered into force in July, 1948. The Surgical Safety Checklist. Authors: World Alliance for Patient Safety, 2008.

8. Diller, T., Helmrich, G., Dunning, S., Cox, S., Buchanan, A., and Shappell, S. 2014. The human factors analysis classification system (HFACS) applied to health care. *American Journal of Medical Quality* 29(3):181–190.

Chapter 13

Graphical and Statistical Methods for High Reliability

Histograms

Histograms are one of my favorite graphical depictions of reality or test of reality. Here is what I mean. The Centers for Medicare & Medicaid Services (CMS) publishes data on every quarter that CMS receives from acute care healthcare organizations in an effort to help consumers choose based on quality. These measures are important being evidence based in their correlation with patient outcomes, if not the outcomes themselves, such as measures of mortality. High reliability is dependent on reliable measurement systems that are capable of accurately and precisely measuring performance over time.

Histograms are a valuable tool in measuring the reliability of a measurement system as we see in the true story as follows:

CMS publishes on Hospital Compare, the CMS website that consumers can access to judge the quality of care among healthcare organizations across the United States. One important metric to many of us is the time that it takes for hospitals to flow a patient in the Emergency Department. One key process is from the time that a physician decides that the patient needs to be admitted from an emergency department (ED) visit to the time that the patient departs the ED for an inpatient room. The measure's description and measure ID are admit decision time to ED departure time for admitted patients (ED-2B).

This is also a lesson in why we coach organizations—that it is more useful to set goals based on the organization's performance rather than a *best practice* or *benchmark* from a measurement system that has not been validated as reliable.

Shown in Figure 13.1[1] is a graph of the actual ED-2B times that is published on Hospital Compare and is visible to anyone in the world who wants to see, compare, and perhaps decide which hospital is better for them.

See the dot out beyond 4200? That converts to a median time of 70 hours for an organization to start the transfer of a patient from the ED after a decision to admit him or her. If you were a patient choosing an ED and hospital for timely and

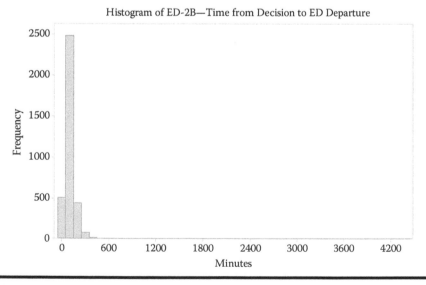

Figure 13.1   Graph of ED-2B admit decision time to ED departure time for admitted patients. (Data from Hospital Compare. Timely and Effective Care, available from the U.S. Health and Human Services at data.medicare.gov.)

effective care, what is the likelihood that you would choose the hospital whose time is supposedly so much longer than the nation's median time of 84 minutes? The 84 minutes is calculated with this data point in the sample.

It seems likely that the measurement system is not reliable, doesn't it? Look at the difference between the median and the mean in a more comprehensive analysis of the same data in Figure 13.2. Using Minitab, we can quickly see a histogram and the descriptive statistics. The median of the population at a 95% confidence level is between 82 and 86. Now, look at the mean and the 20-minute difference that is higher than the median with a confidence interval between 96 and 102.

Most of us would rely more on the median because the data are not normally distributed, which is often the case with time. Also, the data are highly skewed with that one data point.

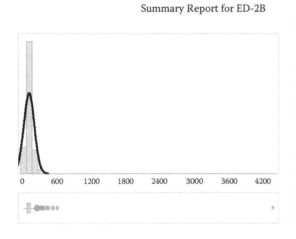

Summary Report for ED-2B

Anderson–Darling normality test	
A-squared	272.27
P-value	<0.005
Mean	99.23
StDev	93.08
Variance	8664.22
Skewness	28.44
Kurtosis	1289.54
N	3498
Minimum	0.00
1st quartile	60.00
Median	84.00
3rd quartile	124.00
Maximum	4388.00
95% confidence interval for mean	
96.15	102.32
95% confidence interval for median	
82.00	86.00
95% confidence interval for StDev	
90.95	95.32

Figure 13.2 **Summary report for ED-2B with descriptive statistics.**

Summary Report for ED-2B

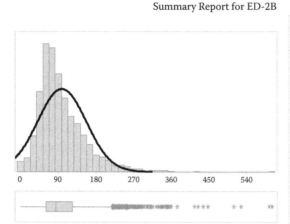

Anderson–Darling normality test	
A-squared	94.57
P-value	<0.005
Mean	98.005
StDev	58.343
Variance	3403.886
Skewness	1.89484
Kurtosis	7.27865
N	3497
Minimum	0.000
1st quartile	60.000
Median	84.000
3rd quartile	123.500
Maximum	601.000
95% confidence interval for mean	
96.070	99.939
95% confidence interval for median	
82.000	86.000
95% confidence interval for StDev	
57.007	59.743

95% confidence intervals

Figure 13.3   After CMS-corrected ED-2B report.

I received a response from CMS, which said that it contacted the organization. I assumed a data error and recalculated the median and mean. In Figure 13.3, one can see that one data point made a difference, and the client received a more reasonable answer to set its goals. Regardless, the lesson learned is to always ensure a reliable measurement system before assuming anything from the data.

Statistical Process Control

Process Control versus Research Batching

Healthcare uses research to find treatments, vaccines, medicines, and a host of solutions in improving our lives and longevity. Perhaps, because of this research and concern for safety, healthcare has struggled to implement process control.

My thoughts are that I am almost always asked what sample size is needed in improvement projects. What I expect to hear before the size of the sample is how do we determine our current capability and if there are any changes occurring?

I do not remember being asked what sample size is needed when starting to collect data in manufacturing quality tracking or in measuring service wait times in the aviation industry—at least not until collecting data and plotting the process output. Healthcare, and more fairly healthcare operations such as in the daily treatment of patients, has not taken advantage of process control data collecting and analysis nearly as well as it has utilized data collecting and analysis for research in the research laboratories.

Why is it important to focus on process control? Simple. Let us go back to the fundamental equation of improvement. Y is a function of the xs coupled with the complexity of healthcare's many processes and variability within those processes. To get the outcome that we expect (the Y), we manage and control the inputs (the xs). Variation is possible throughout time, and therefore we benefit by seeing this variation as it is occurring to manage the x to continue to achieve the Y that is desired. Running healthcare day to day is a constantly changing environment. In research, it is about control. Therefore, research is a *batch* process, and healthcare operations is a flow process.

Batch processes gather things, while no output is achieved until later. In research, scientists perform perfect experimental designs where they plan experiments very carefully, decide the data to collect, collect the data under very controlled environments (control group and treatment group), change the inputs perhaps, collect more data, analyze the data, and then the output comes—findings with all the assumptions and caveats about the experiment and data. The output may be obtained years after data collection. Whereas in running healthcare operations, patients would go nuts after we collect some data, we did not do something, especially in a medical emergency.

Research is to understand our world, and process control is to achieve a better world or at least manage our world.

Which brings me to another question that I often get in healthcare that I did not hear as much outside of healthcare. "Don't we need a control group in a double-blind study?" The answer in healthcare improvement is usually "No."

I believe that one reason healthcare improvement teams have shied away from data and analysis unfortunately is the misunderstanding between research and process control. When Mark Chassin, the president of The Joint Commission, hired me, he purposely avoided the Six Sigma that healthcare was taught by consultants who did not understand healthcare. He knew that Six Sigma outside healthcare worked and was the methodology of choice in many companies. I came to understand his point as I listened to healthcare-trained organizations talk about measuring and remeasuring. This is not Six Sigma. This is healthcare's confusion about sample sizes that are needed for higher confidence in research validity versus healthcare's need for ongoing sampling in real time for process control—virtually infinite sample sizes. Yes, research data collection is a batch that ends, and then conclusions are drawn and reported. Process control is continuous sampling that goes on as long as variation is possible—often forever.

The lesson is to be good at both research and process control. And yes, accurate and precise measurement systems in gathering process control data can also be fabulously powerful research data—two birds with one stone. Said another way, the greatest findings in research applied to healthcare processes are worthless if the process control and capability are not achieved.

Leaders: Look for and reward process control charts as you round in your organization.

Suggest process control charts in those processes that are just not achieving consistent performance.

Engineers: Help the providers and staff start and maintain control charts in key processes and how to interpret and then control their input variables that affect the patient's outcomes and experience.

Even better, before starting a new unit or service line, educate and train the staff in how to manage the new service using control charts and capability analyses that are created from the design research and piloting.

An example is in starting a new urgent care center. Surely, the developers have studied the demand throughout the day, the use of equipment and supplies, the possible queues, and the need for staff. Using statistical process control (SPC) charts of the count of patients is possible hour by hour. Showing the demand changes through the day on an SPC chart helps staff manage to the demand to speed treatment and minimize queue time—two of the most important outputs in a patient's experience. The SPC chart of demand should be on a monitor for all staff to see and is usually automated for real-time managing. Even better is to have SPC charts for the common bottleneck process and other key process steps to know early when changes need to occur to keep the flow going.

In some retail stores, management alert staff to prepare to shift to registers x minutes after a large inflow of customers coming into the store. We have all seen how retailers can quickly open and close registers when queues change in front of them. SPC charts can differentiate common demand amounts versus larger numbers of people entering and thus a need for more registers than normal.

SPC Charts for Reliability[2]

Once the process is in statistical control, the first action on the process should be to locate the process on the target. Actions on the system to reduce the variation from common causes are usually required to improve the ability of the process (and its output) to meet specifications consistently.

Sampling Representing the Population and Reality

We already mentioned sample size briefly when describing confusion about research sampling versus process control sampling. The most important point in sampling is not about sample size. Samples must represent the population. If a sample does not represent the population being studied, the sample can be worse than worthless. It can mislead and result in harm.

What if we wanted to reduce surgical site infections (SSIs) in patients undergoing coronary artery bypass graft (CABG) surgery? Let us say that we find that one of the key variables correlating with the probability of an infection is the length of time between completing the graft and closing the wound. And, let us add that we find a statistically significant difference between surgeons and SSIs occurring. We observe that some surgeons do their own closure immediately, and others let fellows finish the procedures and close the wound but only after the attending surgeon is called back in before closure. When someone other than the attending surgeon closes, the total time of the procedure increases and is correlated with a higher probability of an SSI.

Our sampling plan has us sampling five procedures throughout the day for four months and recording the length of time for the procedure and if an SSI occurred. Sounds like a big sample, right? What is missing? Yes, if we do not stratify the sample to include surgeons who close versus delegate closure, we would not be representing the population of procedures regardless of sample size. It is better to understand the most likely variables correlating with the issue that we are studying than to just blindly start collecting a lot of data.

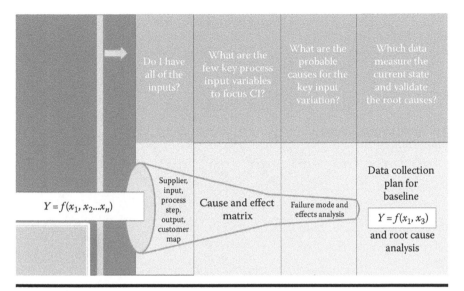

Figure 13.4 Roadmap area showing the filtering of inputs prior to data collecting. CI, continuous improvement.

In our roadmap in Figure 13.4, we do exactly this. We determine the most likely variables first, which allows us to have a higher-quality data collection plan, and often smaller, more efficient sample sizes, and then start sampling.

The trauma from a CABG procedure is significant, and to have an SSI following the procedure is far too common. According to the article "Use of Medicare Claims to Rank Hospitals by Surgical Site Infection Risk Following Coronary Artery Bypass Graft Surgery," between 3% and 9% of patients undergoing a CABG procedure will get infected.[3] In my work at one academic medical center, when I first started the project, I heard that most of the infections were in the leg where the vein is often harvested for the graft. We found that not to be true with 79% of the infections to be in the chest area, not the secondary site.

In Figure 13.5, we use Pareto analysis to find the most common location of an SSI. Organ/space is the most frequent followed by superficial primary, which directs us to the chest area for the most important work to be done.

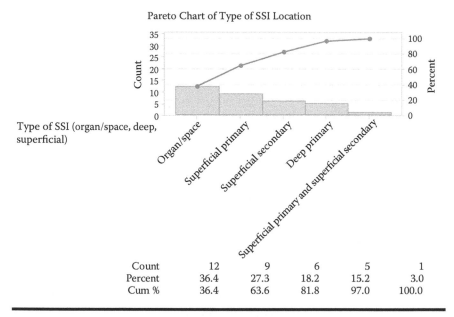

Pareto Chart of Type of SSI Location

	Organ/space	Superficial primary	Superficial secondary	Deep primary	Superficial primary and superficial secondary
Count	12	9	6	5	1
Percent	36.4	27.3	18.2	15.2	3.0
Cum %	36.4	63.6	81.8	97.0	100.0

Figure 13.5 Pareto chart of location of CABG SSI.

SPC in Reliability

SPC in reliability is the *Swiss Army knife* of performance improvement. SPC is *telemetry in intensive care unit*, the DNA test for predisposition to a disease, the critical laboratory result of positive or negative, an alert of change occurring, and the evidence of performance that has improved.

SPC is a high-reliability tool that measures both the outcome and the time. Reliability is equal to getting the expected outcome throughout the expected time.

The story I will share is how we discovered that women were more likely to have a sternal wound infection than men. To begin the story, understand another dimension of performance improvement that I deal with in nearly every engagement and was mentioned before. Throwing someone else's *solutions* at unknown or invalidated root causes is usually less than worthless. Implementing ideas without knowing the root causes wastes time and may endanger patients.

On my first day visiting the cardiothoracic team, I heard the team share proudly that they are now clipping the patient's chest and leg earlier on the floor vs. later in Pre-Op. The pre-operative team members were happy that the process now is taking place earlier on the unit floor by floor staff instead of in the *hurried* environment and the time right before surgery. They went on to explain that this should reduce infections that are caused by clipping.

There are contradicting thoughts in research on the benefit of clipping that is closer to the time of incision. There is also no evidence that clipping earlier reduces infection risk. Thus, the team tried something expecting a reduction in infections, yet they did not have the ability to measure a change nor had they set up a fundamental requirement of experimentation to know if clipping on the floors would have any impact on infections.

In high-reliability organizations (HROs), going back to the teaching of Shewhart and Deming in their plan–do–study–act (PDSA) and plan–do–check–act improvement methods, one plans an experiment by first determining a baseline to know if change occurs. The team then pilots the change and then checks what effect occurred, if any. Two elements were missing in this academic center's experimental design: (1) A baseline other than knowing the overall rate of CABG SSIs monthly and (2) a measurement system to know if the clipping timing and location had an effect.

Leadership lesson: Ask what experiments are being considered, and assist teams in defining clearly the experimental purpose stating clearly the defect or variation being studied before they experiment. Ask them what measure is being used and the reliability of the measurement system in seeing if a change occurs—and how much of a change. Then, ask what root causes are driving them to try this experiment. Ensure that they have stated a hypothesis based on a root cause—not one like this: "Well, someone else said that this would work." If this sounds like Define, Measure, Analyze, Improve, Control (DMAIC) that is associated with Motorola's Six Sigma, it is and for a good reason. Bill Wilson and Mikel Harry used experimental design as they improved the reliability of Motorola's products. The acronym DMAIC explained a simply good experimental design in which PDSA is a core method within a more complete process in reliability improvement. Why would anyone debate the value of defining, measuring, analyzing, improving, and then controlling processes to achieve reliability? I think that life would be simpler, and we prove that reliability gets better when we quit with the "recipe madness" and simply follow DMAIC, which encompasses PDSA and puts PDSA in context with experimental design and process control to achieve the outcomes.

HROs focus on the *x*s to get the *Y*. Hoping for a specific outcome without measuring the performance of the *x*s occurs too often in healthcare. Examples abound with the search for the *best practice* only to frustrate those who try this practice resulting in no significant or sustained improvement. The reason is that healthcare is complex. And, one definition of complexity is the uniqueness of the set of root causes across sites. To throw one site's reported solution at your organization is only a *shot in the dark* without knowing the root causes in your site. Something as simple as hand hygiene is solved differently unit to unit within the same hospital. In an ED or PACU bay separated by curtains, putting alcohol-based hand sanitizers on a wall is not easy enough for the caregivers passing between curtains where a dispenser on a wall is not in the workflow path. Thus, a bedside-mounted dispenser may be more effective.

True, there are variables that are often correlated with CABG SSIs, such as age, gender, and postoperative care after discharge such as poor nutrition and poor wound care. But, we have not always found the body mass index level at mid to middle upper range to be a statistically significant correlation with SSIs.

G Charts

Reliability requires us to continue to measure, but the frequency of failure is very low. A G chart is an SPC chart that is specifically designed to measure and monitor events that happen infrequently. A T chart is similar, and I will explain the differences and when to use each.

I will share actual data from a project to reduce SSIs and how the team used G charts to understand the quality level and later to ensure that higher reliability is sustained.

The G chart in Figure 13.6 shows the days between infections. Each infection is recorded in a column by simply recording the date that the infection occurred or the date of the procedure. Either way, we see the count of infections and in time series order. High reliability will be seen in fewer data

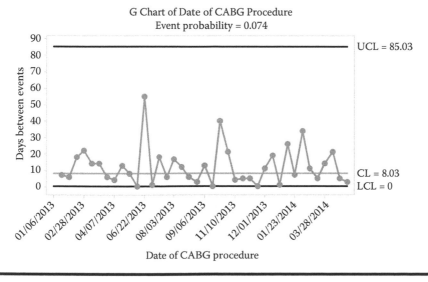

Figure 13.6   G chart of CABG SSIs.

points for the same period of time and data points that are higher on the chart. The reason the points will be higher on the G chart is that the y-axis is the count of days between infections. As the reliability increases, the days between failures also increase. In Figure 13.6, we see the baseline number of days between infections. And, one will notice that the most recent infections may suggest that they started becoming less frequent by looking at the days between when they started increasing. In the second later chart, Figure 13.7, a chart similar to what actually occurred, it is clearer that the reliability improved with the statistical test of 1 infection occurring 3 standard deviations from the center line. On the last infection, we are 95% confident that the days between infections have significantly increased demonstrating higher reliability.

G charts are useful when studying rare events. Considering that HROs have few events, the G chart is often used within HROs. Here is how to read this popular chart that is used by HROs to measure reliability—an SPC chart for rare events.

The time scale on the x-axis is the date of the procedure of the patient who incurred an SSI, although in time series order,

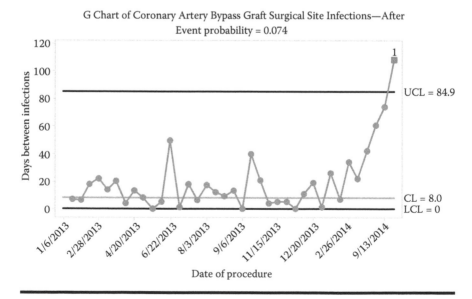

Figure 13.7   Improve phase chart of CABG SSIs.

a date is plotted only if an infection occurred. On the y-axis, we plot the days between procedures when a patient had an SSI. We of course want the plotted points to be higher on the SPC chart signifying more days between procedures resulting in an infection. The mean days between SSIs have been 8.03 days.

The upper control limit suggests that infections are expected to be spaced between the lower bound of zero days and 85 days.

We applied Six Sigma successfully to increase the days between infections, eventually showing a special-cause trend that one can see starting around December. I removed the name of the organization and changed the dates, but the data are from an actual successful reduction effort. The team was under pressure from its state for having one of the highest rates of SSIs and had struggled for years to actually improve.

With the dedication and support of the chief quality officer (CQO), the chief medical officer (CMO), the chair of the department, and every single surgeon and staff member, we identified the root causes, developed solutions, and used the chart in Figure 13.7 daily to assess which solutions worked. Those solutions targeted the variables that are most correlated with SSIs of the chest wound area.

Although some causes are not controllable such as gender, the team developed more robust processes of care regardless. HROs do not give up if they cannot control something such as gender propensity to issues. They drill deeper into the contributing factors that one gender is more likely to receive an infection and then build in more robust treatments to counter the root causes.

T Charts

Use a T chart when the data are the date and time of the events, the elapsed time between events, or the number of intervals between events. See Figure 13.8a and b.

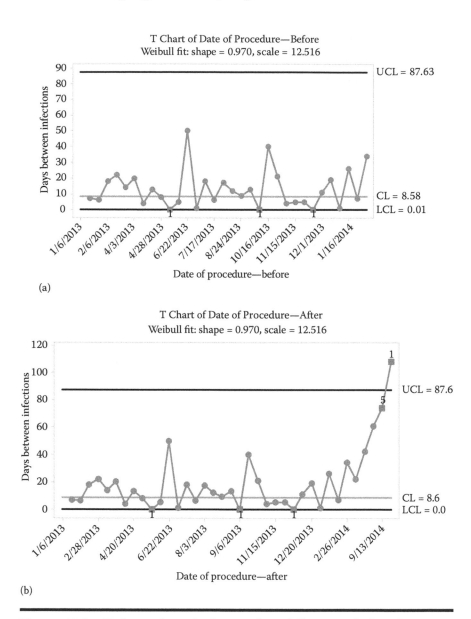

(a)

(b)

Figure 13.8   T chart of surgical procedure failures (a) before improvement and (b) after improvements.

References

1. Hospital Compare. Timely and effective care, available from the U.S. government Health and Human Services at data.medicare .gov.
2. *Statistical Process Control Reference Manual*, Automotive Industry Action Group. Second Edition (Second Edition issued July 2005 © 1992, 1995, 2005 DaimlerChrysler Corporation, Ford Motor Company, and General Motors Corporation ISBN # 978-1-60534-108-8).
3. Available at http://www.cdc.gov/nchs/nvss.htm.

Chapter 14

Financial Impact as High Reliability Is Achieved

The Cost of Poor Quality

Illingworth et al. in the *American Journal of Medical Quality* found a strong, statistically significant correlation in Louisiana and Texas as quality improves in the quality improvement measures, the xs, and a reduction in the frequency of medical liability claims.[1] In Figure 14.1, we see the inflection point when quality improvement is correlated with a significant reduction in the frequency of liability claims. In early 2003, Louisiana hospitals began achieving higher mean scores in Centers for Medicare & Medicaid Services (CMS) quality measures. In this same time frame, the mean monthly claims started reducing. By 2006, the organizations were achieving nearly zero defects in compliance to evidence-based process measures and benefitting from the lowest mean monthly claims from approximately a mean of 4.5 to 2.5.

I have yet had a Chief Financial Officer (CFO) volunteer this cost of poor quality in our value to the client. Cost accounting is a measurement system. We have learned in this book and my previous books that we should analyze the accuracy and

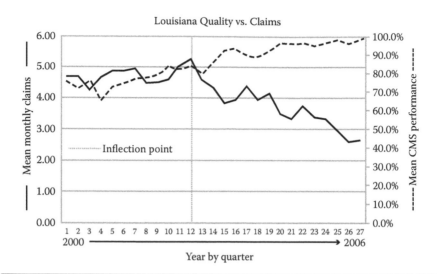

Figure 14.1   Louisiana quality versus claims and inflection point. (From The Commonwealth Fund Report, Mirror, Mirror on the Wall, 2014. Update: How the U.S. Health Care System Compares Internationally. Available at http://www.commonwealthfund.org/publications/fund -reports/2014/jun/mirror-mirror, 2014.)

precision of measurement systems before we rely on what the measurement system tells us. We must do the same in cost accounting.

Harley-Davidson found way back in the 1980s that its cost accounting was not accurately accounting all the costs from poor quality. And, they were driving wrong behaviors reducing quality and thus profitability even more. Harley started identifying the correlation between higher-warranty costs and diminishing sales with lower quality. They discovered that they had to change the accounting equation. Once they stopped overfocusing on direct labor and underfocusing on rework (repeated patient tests, do-over surgical procedures) and all the costs of returned product and field repair (patient readmissions), and lost sales (lost referrals by providers), they turned the corner on profitability.

Harley became the showcase of higher reliability as well as employee satisfaction and competitive advantage and how to recapture the customer loyalty and profit recovery. Harley motorcycles had become the butt of jokes that Harleys left their mark on each parking spot—oil leaks from highly unreliable quality.

Activity-Based Costing in Healthcare

Activity-based costing (ABC) is now being elevated in healthcare as it was in manufacturing starting in the 1980s. ABC calculates the cost of a service more accurately than the traditional cost accounting, which pools the overhead expenses and then allocates back to the cost of the service based on one variable such as direct labor regardless of the amount of other labor, equipment, and overhead supplies that are used by the service. When overhead is high, as in most healthcare organizations that provide surgical care and other complex procedures, ABC can be much more accurate than traditional methods. ABC has been around since 1981 and the traditional cost accounting perhaps a hundred years before.[2]

ABC allocates the costs of a service based on the service's consumption of resources, such as the actual time that physicians, nurses, therapists, and others provide during the service and the time that was consumed in the capital equipment time. (Think imaging equipment.) In traditional costing, finance sums the overhead costs and then allocates the costs to services or products based on direct labor hours or cubic feet. In ABC, the amount of provider time, imaging time, nursing time, and other resources would be totaled to cost the service. Generally, ABC costing is more accurate when high overhead costs exist and better accuracy is valued.

High-reliability organizations also benefit from accurately knowing their costs. One reason is that they can focus on improvement efforts for the largest financial gain. Increasing margins may allow the organizations to devote more resources to improving reliability even more. Losing money and decreasing reliability can go hand in hand. I reach out to healthcare organizations that are very low performers in quality and their patients' experiences, and they want help. However, they are *bleeding cash* and struggling just to stay open. Paying for outside help, which is desperately needed because they do not have the money to pay for their own resources, is very difficult. Making their matters worse, the healthcare organizations that are excelling in reliability and whose patients and providers recommend may be achieving higher margins, growing cash, and increasing their race in reliability and even higher margins by contracting with outside firms that bring in expertise.

Pay for Quality and Reliability

CMS adds fuel to the fire when it incentivizes healthcare organizations through its value-based purchasing (VBP) program paying incentive to those healthcare organizations that are already above the national median in performance and penalizing those that are below average. Blue Cross Blue Shield of Massachusetts (BCBSMA) has its Alternative Quality Contract (see Figure 14.2) that in 2015 is paying up to a 5% incentive based on quality.[3]

In healthcare today, the competition is increasing, and decisions are more and more based on costs across competing organizations. Walmart has requested quotes for common services and uses quality and cost as major determinants. A healthcare organization that knows its costs for the service may be much more likely to win the business compared to one that allocates incorrectly the high overhead costs to the service that is under proposal. Either way, too much allocation or too little, the healthcare organization will suboptimize the margin. If the organization allocates too much overhead to the service and thus quotes higher than needed for an expected margin, an organization with all other variables that are equal will quote a lower price. If

BCBSMA—large upside for quality. VBP measures include outcomes and patient experience like CMS VBP

The Alternative Quality Contract

Global budget
- Population-based budget covers full care continuum
- Health status adjusted
- Based on historical claims
- Shared risk (2-sided)
- Trend targets set at baseline for multi-year

Quality incentives
- Ambulatory and hospital
- Significant earning potential
- Nationally accepted measures
- Continuum of performance targets for each measure (good to great)

Add this to the 2% incentive from VBP

Long-term contract
- 5-year agreement
- Sustained partnership
- Supports ongoing investment and commitment to improvement

Figure 14.2   BCBSMA alternative quality contract. Commonwealth Fund Webinar with slides provided by BCBSMA, 2015.

the organization underallocates the overhead and thus shares a lower price to the customers, it could actually be providing services under the expected margin and perhaps at a loss.

Robert S. Kaplan and Steven R. Anderson wrote that "With good estimates of the typical path an individual patient takes for a medical condition, providers can use the time-driven activity-based costing system to assign costs accurately and relatively easily to each process step along the path."[4] This improved version of ABC requires that providers estimate only two parameters at each process step: the cost of each of the resources used in the process and the quantity of time that the patient spends with each resource.[2]

Population Health—What It May Really Mean in the Future

David Kindig and Greg Stoddart in their paper, "What Is Population Health?," define population health as "the health outcomes of a group of individuals, including the distribution of such outcomes within the group." These populations are often geographic regions, such as nations or communities, but they can also be other groups, such as employees, ethnic groups, disabled persons, or prisoners. Such populations are of relevance to policy makers. In addition, many determinants of health, such as medical care systems, the social environment, and the physical environment, have their biological impact on individuals in part at a population level.[5]

The Institute for Healthcare Improvement's (IHI's) Triple Aim[6] created originally by Don Berwick, Tom Nolan, and John Whittington is to simultaneously improve population health, improve the patient experience of care, and reduce per-capita cost. The Triple Aim began in 2008 with a purpose to fundamentally develop new health systems that contribute to the overall health of populations while reducing costs. The U.S. National Quality Strategy and other organizations outside of the United States have been included in the development of the Triple Aim.

On July 1, 2015, Health Secretary Jeremy Hunt, in a speech to the Local Government Association annual conference, shared, "I want Britain to be the best country in the world to grow old in."[7]

Hunt challenged Britain's citizens to do their part in caring for their elderly while also keeping costs down. Both the National Health Service (NHS) and the Triple Aim emphasize measurement as key. The NHS has recently made surgeon outcomes transparent—a remarkable change and one that supports patients and families taking on responsibility to improve healthcare and reinforces those that achieve higher reliability. Who would go to a surgeon, if the choice exists, who has the lowest-quality outcomes?

The IHI goes on to suggest that the measures used in its Triple Aim also define what is meant by population health. The Triple Aim initiative is based on improving three sets of measures and thus improving our population's health. The IHI believes that focusing on these measures can potentially lead us to better models for providing healthcare. The sets are the following:

1. Improve the health of the defined population
2. Enhance the patient care experience (including quality, access, and reliability)
3. Reduce, or at least control, the per-capita cost of care

Accounting for the cost and financial returns from improving population health is entirely consistent with achieving higher reliability. Calculating the cost of poor quality could well include the measures in the Triple Aim because these measures include both clinical outcomes that are important to us, the patients, and the costs of harm and death when our healthcare system does not deliver the value. In addition, the death and harm that we ourselves contribute from unhealthy habits such as smoking and obesity are included in the measures.

I see the future of healthcare measures publicly reported in the future to be about clinical functional outcomes. At present, most so-called outcome measures are about healthcare-acquired harm and death. High-reliability organizations can focus much more on serving the customers than on how often they injure the customers or their own employees and visitors.

Matthew C. Stiefel, Rocco J. Perla, and Bonnie L. Zell believe that, "Healthy life expectancy (HLE) is a measure of population health that combines length and quality of life into a single measure."[8] This metric is patient-centric and focused on the outcome of healthcare most people value.

Shown in the following paragraph are measures that healthcare organizations and the public might begin measuring, or perhaps these measures will follow or precede measures based on the availability and maturity of the organization.

The Triple Aim's outcome measures of cost include:

1. *Per-capita cost*: total cost per member of the population per month
2. *Hospital and emergency department utilization rate and/or cost*

Figure 14.3 is a framework of per-capita cost.

The Triple Aim adds measures on the experience of care:

1. *Standard questions from patient surveys, for example,*
   - Global questions from Consumer Assessment of Healthcare Providers and Systems or "How's Your Health?" surveys
   - Likelihood to recommend a set of measures based on key dimensions (e.g., Institute of Medicine's six aims for improvement: safe, effective, timely, efficient, equitable, and patient centered)

And population health measures:

2. Health outcomes
   - *Mortality*: years of potential life lost; life expectancy; standardized mortality ratio
   - *Health and functional status*: single-question assessment (e.g., from Centers for Disease Control [CDC] HRQOL-4) or multidomain assessment (e.g., VR-12, Patient Reported Outcomes Measurement Information System [PROMIS] Global-10)
   - *Healthy life expectancy*: combines life expectancy and health status into a single measure, reflecting the remaining years of life in good health
   - *Disease burden*: incidence (yearly rate of onset, average age of onset) and/or prevalence of major chronic conditions

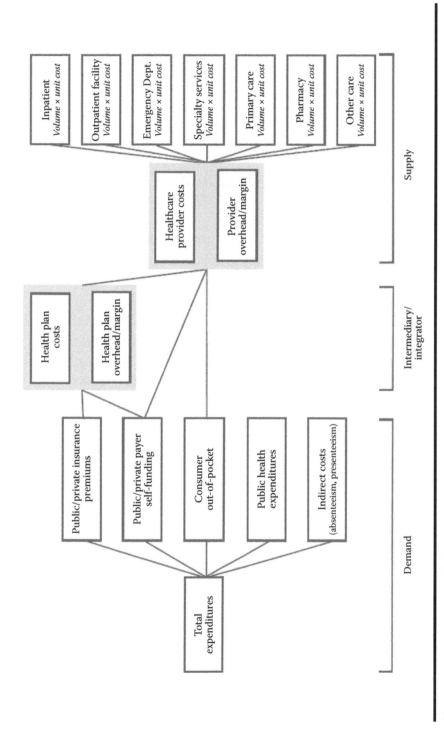

Figure 14.3 Framework of costs.

– *Behavioral and physiological factors*: behavioral factors include smoking, alcohol consumption, physical activity, and diet. Physiological factors include blood pressure, body mass index, cholesterol, and blood glucose (possible measure: a composite health risk assessment score).

Value Stream and the Accountable Care Organizations

A value stream is exactly the concept that I shared in Chapter 12, the chapter showing the rolled throughput yield. For those trained by consultants espousing Lean, I remind readers that mapping the flow of a patient and assessing which activities add value in the mind of a patient and those that do not can help us prioritize waste reduction efforts. In reliability, we are most concerned with preventing failures over the intended time. Lean practitioners often go directly to building the popular value stream map. They have a bias toward measuring time, while cursory attention highlights issues along the way in shapes representing starbursts and potential good ideas in clouds.

What is missing in the popular value stream map are the inputs that contribute to the bursts. Will a map of a value stream work as well as a map that shows the inputs and potential failures along the patient's journey? I do not think so because Y is a function of the xs. High-reliability organizations focus on the inputs and, specifically, the quality of the input and outcome. By reducing the defects caused by the inputs and the interaction of the inputs, waste will be reduced.

Pay for Performance Featuring VBP, Excess Readmissions, Healthcare-Acquired Conditions, and Similar Alternative Quality Contracts (BCBSMA)

Starting with patient discharges from acute care hospitals in October of 2012, CMS for the first time shifted reimbursement away from simply paying for services that are provided regardless of the outcome. The program is named value-based purchasing, and it started incentivizing quality via higher compliance to process measures of care and better patient experiences. In fiscal year 2017, CMS has shifted the weight of the VBP incentives away from the process measures and toward outcome measures (although the outcomes are safety measures such as healthcare-acquired conditions, not clinical function outcomes). CMS has added efficiency measures, specifically the Medicare spending per beneficiary, and has maintained 25% of the weight on the patients' experiences using the Hospital Consumer Assessment of Healthcare Providers and Systems survey process.

VBP was drafted in 2006, well before the Affordable Care Act (ACA), which made it statutory for CMS to begin and control its development. Despite the intense debate over the ACA, the move toward pay for performance has been recognized as positive by those wanting to improve the reliability of healthcare. This includes other payers such as Blue Cross Blue Shield (BCBS). BCBS claims that it has boosted value-based care spending to $71 billion in 2014, which is a 9% increase in claims that are timed to VBP since 2013.[3]

References

1. Illingworth, K. D., Shaha, S. H., Tzeng, T. H., Sinha, M. S., and Saleh, K. J. 2015. The impact of tort reform and quality improvements on medical liability claims: A tale of 2 states. *American Journal of Medical Quality* 30(3): 263–270.
2. Jilani. Difference Between ABC and Traditional Costing. DifferenceBetween.net. Available at http://www.difference between.net/business/finance-business-2/difference-between -abc-and-traditional-costing, 2011.
3. The Commonwealth Fund report, Mirror, Mirror on the Wall, 2014 Update: How the U.S. Health Care System Compares Internationally. Available at http://www.commonwealthfund .org/publications/fund-reports/2014/jun/mirror-mirror, 2014.
4. Kaplan, R. S. and Anderson, S. R. 2004. Time-driven activity-based costing. *Harvard Business Review*, from the November 2004 issue.
5. Kindig, D. and Stoddart, G. 2003. What is population health? *American Journal of Public Health* 93(3): 380–383.
6. Institute for Healthcare Improvement, Cambridge, MA. Available at http://www.ihi.org/Engage/Initiatives/TripleAim /Documents/BeasleyTripleAim_ACHEJan09.pdf.
7. From: Department of Health and The Rt Hon Jeremy Hunt MP. Delivered on July 1, 2015 (Transcript of the speech, exactly as it was delivered). Location: Harrogate, England. First published: July 1, 2015.
8. Stiefel, M. C., Perla, R. J., and Zell, B. L. 2010. A healthy bottom line: Healthy life expectancy as an outcome measure for health improvement efforts. *The Milbank Quarterly* 88(1): 30–53.

Chapter 15

Conclusions

No margin—no mission—is perhaps the most accepted truth of healthcare. Competing in reliability can be the difference between financial failure and a healthcare system having the profits, growth, and provider and patient loyalty to scale its methods across the globe. Ford achieved a reliable automobile design and manufacturing process that the world benefitted from and Toyota emulated and improved upon. As James Womack shared in his book *The Machine That Changed the World* (1990), Toyota took Ford's highly reliable design and manufacturing process and became the manufacturer of some of the most reliable automobiles in the world. And, according to Womack, this reliability provided the ability of *Leaning* out processes across the business resulting in the most-profitable high-volume car manufacturer in the world.

Consultants who suggest that leaders in the automotive, electrical safety, aviation, and aerospace and first responder communications achieve their competitive advantage without the concepts in this book are causing healthcare's slowness in achieving high reliability. They oversimplify the tools and techniques that are required. Oversimplification, per James Reason in his book *Human Error* (1990), is one of the most dangerous traits in achieving the quality, safety, reliability, and customer loyalty that high-reliability organizations enjoy.

I believe that there will be healthcare organizations that achieve reliable patient outcomes with zero defects over the years. We are achieving zero defects of process measures, the xs of health outcomes. By achieving fewer defects in our healthcare processes, we will improve the probability of reliable outcomes.

What can be more important for us humans to achieve than our own quality of life? Even the best hospitals, clinics, ambulatory surgical centers, skilled nursing facilities, or population health ventures have defect rates that achieve zero defects on all but the fewest services and products for the expected life. To be fair, Ford's Model T was a vastly simpler entity than we humans. No car has achieved the reliability of our lives with some fortunate humans lasting a lifetime without major surgery or illness until passing. But, God designed us.

Thankfully, we in healthcare are only competing against fellow humans. Improving healthcare reliability together for shared learning holds the greatest promise for humankind's desire to improve the reliability of our lives. We will achieve higher reliability in health over longer and longer times using these methods and working together.

Thank you for reading this book, and best wishes in applying the lessons that you have learned from it. We will all benefit.

May God bless you.

Rick Morrow

Index